HOW I PROVED LIFE AFTER DEATH

HOW I PROVED LIFE
AFTER DEATH

Wendy Marston

Book Guild Publishing
Sussex, England

First published in Great Britain in 2015 by
The Book Guild Ltd
The Werks
45 Church Road
Hove, BN3 2BE

This book is a work of non-fiction based on the life, experiences and
recollections of the author. In some cases names of people and places
have been changed solely to protect the privacy of others. The author
has stated to the publishers that, except in such minor respects not
affecting the substantial accuracy of the work, the contents of this
book are true.

The author and publishers do not dispense medical advice or assume
responsibility for any adverse conditions or actions discussed in this book.
The advice of a medical doctor should always be sought regarding any
medical condition.

Typesetting in Times by
Ashford Colour Press Ltd, Cheshire

Printed and bound in Great Britain by
CPI Group (UK) Ltd, Croydon, CR0 4YY

A catalogue record for this book is available from
The British Library.

ISBN 978 1 909984 74 5

*I would like to dedicate this book to Janice.
Without your message from the spirit world I would
never have put pen to paper.*

Contents

1

London

If I hadn't accidentally locked myself in my bedroom all day, I may never have proved life after death.

It was 1965, and the place to be in the 1960s was said to be London. I shared a top-floor maisonette in Belsize Park with three other girls. We were a motley crew. Diane, slim and blonde, was a northern lass from the Lake District, who played hockey in her spare time. She was really the leader of the pack, freshly out of university and working in the Green Park area. Sophie was slim with short dark hair, and was brought up in France. She was the feisty one in the house, as the milkman found out to his cost when he was inconsistent with the milk deliveries. Margaret was short, not fat, but more rounded than the other two. Her hair was cut in a short bob which suited her, and she was so well turned out – she always looked neat and sweet. We all worked in various office jobs. I was regarded as the lucky one, as I worked for a firm of solicitors in the City.

Our accommodation was spread over the top two floors of an elderly end of terrace house. All the houses were in rows, back to back, and it was very much flat-dwellers' territory in those days. It was winter time, and all the other girls had left for work. As I didn't start work until ten o'clock I had the last turn in the bathroom and, to keep the bedroom warm, shut the bedroom door while I dressed. On this particular day when I was ready for work, I pulled the door handle down to open the door, and then snap, I was left with the handle in my hand, and the door firmly shut. The door had been needing a good tug to get it to open for some time, but being young we hadn't reported it to the landlord, or given it a second thought.

I stared at the door for a minute or two, trying to come up with one of my cunning plans, but nothing I tried seemed to work. I tried fiddling the lock with a metal comb, trying to hook things through the little gap between the door and the floor, and then finally charging at the door with a chair. It was so tightly stuck in the frame that nothing I did would make it budge. I looked out of the window at the back of the building, I opened it and tried yelling 'Help!' but everyone around had left for work long ago. I had no next-door neighbours as we were on the end of the terrace, and our own staircase was on the other side of the room. I contemplated knotting strips of sheet together, and lowering myself to the ground, but one look at the long drop to the ground made me realise that could end in disaster.

In those days we didn't have the luxury of mobile phones, and in the bedroom no landline phone, and certainly no television or radio. I knew Margaret would be the first one home at six o'clock that evening, so I had to face the fact I was in for a thirsty, hungry, boring day. I looked at the wardrobe, and my chest of drawers, and decided I would give them a good old turn out. I took everything out, and began to rearrange things to keep my mind occupied, and away from thoughts of lovely cups of steaming hot coffee!

In a far corner I found a rather tatty paperback book. I can't remember the title, but I think it was written by a medium called Ena Twigg. I snuggled underneath my bed covers, and spent most of the day reading the book. That was the first seed that was firmly planted in my head about the Spirit World. It didn't answer all the questions I had kept asking the vicar at confirmation classes about what people did in heaven all day, but it did start me on a whole new train of thought.

Margaret's key turned in the lock at six o'clock and I have never been so grateful to hear that sound as I was that day. I started shouting, 'Margaret, Margaret, let me out!' and banging my fist on the door. I was like a wild animal. I couldn't stop to explain to a poor bemused Margaret as I raced past her to get to the kitchen. I can remember opening a tin of mushroom soup at speed, and putting it in a pan on the gas hob. Mushroom soup had never tasted so good. Diane and Sophie came home, and the story of my imprisonment was met with howls of laughter.

The next day I had to face my boss, and all my office colleagues. The laughter started all over again. Colleagues told me how worried they had been, because they knew it wasn't like me: they knew I always phoned if I was ill.

One by one people were coming up to me saying, 'How did you manage without a toilet for a whole day?'

My answer to that was, 'Next time you buy a waste paper bin, don't buy one of those basket type ones, make sure you get a tin one!'

After lunch that day, and having relived the drama with the other girls in the office, I returned to my desk. There on my typewriter was a bar of very dark chocolate. It had a little note on it from my long-suffering boss, Mr Murrell, and it read 'Wendy's Iron Ration'.

My office was in the Chamber of Shipping building, and the solicitors I worked for were known as shipping solicitors. We shared the building with various other companies all connected with shipping.

At that time the secretarial team was made up of a couple of spinster ladies, a couple of older married ladies, and then there were about five of us young girls. The youngest, and most angelic-looking one of us, had short blonde hair and pale, very beautiful white skin. Named Geraldine she lived at home with her parents, and spent her weekends immersed in Salvation Army activities. She would often show us photos of herself wearing her Salvation Army bonnet, which she wore when attending meetings with other members of her family. Her face just screamed innocence.

We didn't have any kind of rest room, or kitchen, or indeed in those days not even a coffee machine. We were allowed a short break mid-morning to pop round the corner to the local coffee shop. We had our fairly regular times for walking round in little groups, and most of us younger girls, if we were not taking dictation, would walk round together.

When I started working there the builders were carrying out alterations. They were working on the staircases, and the very antique-looking lift, with a wrought iron gate across the front. Our entry was up a staircase with boarding along one side. One morning a small round hole appeared in the boarding, very innocent-looking, and not even noticed by most people.

The next morning Geraldine asked if any of us had seen anything strange poking through the hole in the boarding by the stairs. We all looked at one another and said, 'What sort of thing?' None of us could recall seeing anything. She said that every time she went past the hole something would poke out. She had told her mother, and her mother had said she was to go and tell the senior partner's secretary, as she was a married lady. She wanted to know what we thought. A lot of glances were exchanged, and the giggles began as we decided to drink up our coffee and investigate the scene of the crime. We took turns to walk up and down past the hole, but nothing happened. We did, however, spot another hole higher up.

Geraldine must have had her word with the senior partner's secretary, as soon the office gossip was buzzing with the story that one of the builders was exposing himself through the hole in the boarding. It seemed it was only targeted at Geraldine. The young male clerks were having a field day with their suggestions of how to solve the problem, the favoured option being to supply all female staff with indelible ink pens. As soon as they saw anything, they were to mark it with a pen. An identity parade of builders would then reveal the culprit!

All the nonsense kept everyone amused for a few days, and then the hole was filled in. It was rumoured that the senior partner had spoken to the head of the building company, and that was the end of the hysteria.

It was a fun office to work for in those days. We worked hard, but we all had time for jokes and laughter. We had a lovely widow lady who bustled around with lots of jangling bracelets, so you always knew who was approaching. She was the receptionist and telephonist. We all called her Cassie, as her name was Mrs Cassington. She had neat grey hair, permed so that it always looked very curly, and in those days we would have described her as plump. She dressed in loose dresses, and always wore high-heeled shoes that made a click clack sound when she walked down the corridor. She had a keen sense of humour and loved to tell jokes, but at the same time she was very caring and motherly with the younger girls.

I remember the day when my father phoned the office to tell me my beloved grandfather had died. I was round at the coffee shop. On my return Cassie was very careful to take me to one side and break the news as gently as possible.

The switchboard was an old fashioned 'doll's eye' board, where you had pegs on leads, and every time there was an incoming call, you put a peg in the hole. This pushed the doll's eye lid back into the board. It wasn't the most reliable system in the world, and the telephone engineers were frequent visitors. After a few visits I think they caught the jovial atmosphere of the office. They became as up for a laugh as the rest of us. They asked Cassie if she had oiled the doll's eyes lately. She took it seriously, and when they left she carefully poured oil into each little hole. The outcome of course was total chaos, and the switchboard was a complete write-off. Being a firm of solicitors I think there were a lot of angry letters, and threats to sue, flying around. A smart new board was installed that didn't have any holes, or doll's eyes. Cassie lived to tell the tale and learnt to work the new shiny plastic board. She was a lovely lady, and we all thought the world of her. Very many years later, when she was in her late eighties, I learnt she had died in her sleep.

I shared an office with a spinster lady, a good 30 years older than myself, and she was affectionately known as Auntie Oli, as her name was Olive. She always looked smart, and wore mainly rich-coloured suits, or dresses, that covered her ample figure. She visited the hairdressers every Saturday, and her grey wavy hair had a blue rinse, as it was termed in the 1960s. She had a round face with rosy cheeks, and a mischievous twinkle in her eye. Every lunchtime she would cover her desk with serviettes, and bring out her cracker biscuits, cucumber and oranges. Our office always smelt of oranges, but everyone knew it was Auntie Oli's staple diet. A great stickler for routine, she would walk to Petticoat Lane each Friday lunch time to top up her supplies of oranges and cucumbers. Auntie Oli was a really good sport. She liked nothing better than playing with her next-door neighbour's children. She thought it was an absolute hoot the day she jumped into their paddling pool, slipped up, and ended up flat on her back, soaked to the skin.

As I remember all the fun and the pranks in that office, I think apologies are in order. I am sorry, Mr Williams, that I glued the pages of your newspaper together. I am sorry that I filled your umbrella with the clippings from the hole punch gadget, and I do apologise for sticking spiky hair rollers inside your bowler hat.

After six happy years working in the City, all the younger secretaries were beginning to get married, and move on to the next stage of their lives. I was no exception, and newly married, John and I decided to move out of London. John's office was near Euston station, so we kept house-hunting along the railway line until we reached a town that had an acceptable commute, and where the houses were affordable. We settled on Leighton Buzzard as it had good rail links to London, and in those days was a small market town just beginning to expand. There were lots of new houses being built, and the new city of Milton Keynes was on the drawing board. We moved out of London and into Leighton Buzzard on a very hot August day.

Our daughter, Annabelle, was born, and we acquired a very adorable bouncy golden retriever puppy, who was named Rupert. As young couples do, we adjusted to parenthood and a new lifestyle, and then baby number two was on the way. Annabelle was a happy little three-year old and attended a local nursery school in the mornings. I had made friends with the other mothers at the school, and we used to help one another with child-minding. Such things as hospital appointments and so on were easier without the children in tow. It was in these circumstances that I was looking after a friend's child who became very unwell in my care. It turned out to be mumps, and predictably, not long afterwards Annabelle developed the mumps. By this time I was seven months pregnant. It hadn't entered my head that I might catch it myself. I awoke one morning with a very swollen painful face, and immediately thought I must have an abscess under a tooth. It was so excruciatingly painful that I remember getting myself dressed and straight down to the doctor before the surgery opened. The GP recognised it as mumps straight away, and sent me away with antibiotics.

It became obvious that I had a very nasty case of the mumps, contracting it in adulthood, and we sent for my parents to come and stay to help with Annabelle and Rupert. Fortunately my father had just retired, so they drove the 125 miles from Lymington to take charge. They had been staying with us for Christmas, and had only been home for a couple of weeks, so they loaded the car once again and came to our aid.

I was in bed with a very high temperature and fever, and the first thing my mother did was to send for the doctor. This time a new doctor in the practice came out, and I recognised her at once. She was one of the other mothers with small children at the nursery school. Caroline was very concerned about me, and the fact that I was heavily pregnant. She took me off the antibiotics, and said it was only a case of trying to keep my temperature as low as possible.

It shouldn't have been difficult to keep me cool, as the January winter was sharp. The snow was starting to fall, and by night we were having heavy frosts. It was a particularly difficult winter. The press had nicknamed it the 'Winter of Discontent'. The Council gritting lorries were nowhere to be seen, as the drivers were on strike. The train drivers were also on strike, so there were terrible transport problems. The petrol tanker drivers had been refusing to deliver petrol to the garages, and the ancillary nurses were on strike in the hospitals.

My fever just seemed to go from bad to worse. I started to hallucinate from time to time. I remember waking in the morning to the sound of a blizzard, with snow beating against the windows. My husband was just waking and wondering how he was going to get into his office in London. The radio was telling people to stay indoors unless their journey was essential. Downstairs my parents were preparing breakfast, feeding the dog and so on. And then it happened. My waters broke.

I had another six weeks or so to go before the birth, and I didn't know what to think about first. How were we going to get to the hospital? Annabelle's delivery had been a tricky one in the operating theatre, and I had been told in no uncertain terms that a home delivery was out of the question. All John kept saying was, 'You can't be serious.'

My mother, practical as ever, filled a flask with hot drink, threw sandwiches together and gathered blankets. John phoned the hospital, and was told to set off and take me in. For some reason we took my little old red Mini, which we always referred to as 'half-timbered'. I think we must have thought it would perform better on the ice than the big old family estate car. Progress was very slow through the traffic. The lorries were having difficulty with the hills, and the cars were only creeping along. Fortunately I wasn't having contractions, but I was still in a lot of pain from the mumps, and just wanted to be curled up in bed. I was also very frightened, and filled with disbelief that this could be happening to us.

Eventually we made it to the hospital in Luton, but instead of the usual half an hour, the journey had taken us something like three hours. There weren't many nurses to be seen in the maternity unit, but we were ushered into an enormous delivery

9

room. There was only one chair and I sat down while John tried to thaw out by the radiator. After waiting for what seemed a very long time they did get me on the ugly trolley bed on wheels. It had been decided that I was to be hooked up to the drip machine to induce the baby, and get my contractions going. At the sight of needles and drips John decided it was time he fled. He needed to get started on the return journey home, as the snow was still falling thick and fast.

The nurse who had been getting me established on the drip explained they only had one Sister, and a few nurses, on duty in the whole maternity unit. They had something like six mothers giving birth at the same time, no doctors, and as they were on strike, no staff in the kitchen preparing food. The nurses were doing their best, dispensing cups of tea and toast. I was given my call button on a cable, and the nurse disappeared. I was all alone and trying to keep calm as the contractions started. The nurse would pop in every half an hour, and disappear again. The contractions started to get stronger and I pressed my call button. I could hear all the other bells ringing down the corridor, and nobody was coming. Eventually a nurse did come, and scolded me for calling, saying it would be ages yet before the baby was born. She left me, and I was feeling pretty desolate. The snow was still beating against the window, the wind was howling, and here I was in the middle of this enormous plain white room, with areas of open space around me, and no humans in sight.

The contractions began to get a lot stronger, and I was feeling the urge to push. I needed a nurse. I pressed my bell, and nobody came. It must have been about five minutes later, but seemed an age to me, when a rather cross-looking nurse did appear.

'I have told you it will be ages yet,' she snapped – then she saw the baby appearing. She fiddled around with a thin polythene apron, chastising me for not giving her time to put it on!

It was now 6.30 in the evening as baby Freddie was born. Considering he was early, he wasn't too bad a weight at 6 lb 6 oz. Once Freddie had been attended to, he was put into his see-through box on wheels, and both of us were taken to our own room. We were wheeled by female nurses, and didn't pass another living soul on our way. By the time they had settled me into my bed, and given me tea and toast, I was beginning to feel as if I had the plague!

My consultant came to visit us the next day, and I greeted him with a sarcastic comment about men not being brave enough to darken my door, in case they caught mumps. He was at pains to explain he hadn't been able to get to Luton from Stevenage through the snow. Stepping back closer to the door, he was protesting it was nothing to do with the fact I had the mumps. Twenty-four hours later, baby and I were discharged.

Those early days were not easy. I was still extremely poorly with the mumps. I was trying to recover from giving birth, and I had a baby who wouldn't stop crying. My long-suffering parents must have been exhausted themselves, looking after a three-year-old, a young dog, and doing the shopping and cooking. They were obviously worried about me, and a tiny baby who was having trouble taking his bottles. I can remember how my father paced up and down with Freddie on his shoulder, trying to get him to sleep. After a couple of weeks my parents returned home, and my face had at last resumed its usual shape. I was getting very little sleep, and I felt pretty grim.

The health visitor came and I explained about the feeding problems with the baby. 'The problem is that you had a girl first,' she said. 'This is reality, now you have a boy!' My wonderful next-door neighbour and friend was the only person who seemed to realise how much I was struggling. The first months of Freddie's life were like a nightmare, and then as we moved him onto slightly solid food he started projectile vomiting. We used to say he could hit a moving target at 10 yards!

The regular visits to the clinic for weighing usually proved he was gaining weight, if only slowly, and my pleas for practical suggestions with the feeding were always met with platitudes. The health visitor who had told me I was now facing reality with a boy suggested that if he didn't eat his lunch, I was to put it in the refrigerator until teatime. If I kept serving it up he would get so hungry he would eventually eat it. I gave it a go, but abandoned it to save him from dying of hunger. Instinct told me there was something wrong, but I didn't know what.

In August 1979 we held his christening at the local church, and had a big party for friends and family in the garden. It was a very warm day, and turned out to be a lovely occasion. Both sets of grandparents were there, and we had managed to collect an assorted array of beach chairs and folding tables. One very good friend, a young mum, had the misfortune to sit on an ancient canvas beach chair supplied by my in-laws. The canvas ripped from one end to the other and my friend landed unceremoniously on the hard concrete of the patio. Everyone laughed, and the poor girl had bruises for a long time. I am sure she remembers the incident to this day.

Freddie's cry sounded like the noise an old donkey would make. It was very distinctive. One friend told me many years later that hearing him cry at the christening had sent shivers down her spine. She had heard it before, coming from a baby who was later found to be autistic.

Freddie never did sleep through the night without waking me, until he was four years old. My body adjusted to continually getting up at night, and to this day I can never sleep for any length of time without waking. He began to crawl, and then to walk, and he looked a very normal little toddler. He would never sit in a baby chair without screaming, and constantly wanted to sit with me. He didn't make any of the usual baby gurgling noises that I have since learnt are called babbling. He was just very quiet, apart from crying. He passed all the regular hearing tests at the clinic, but he had started to snore loudly. We were referred by the GP to the Ear, Nose and Throat Department at the hospital, and his adenoids were removed, with grommets being placed in his ears. That solved the snoring problem, but he still wasn't making any attempt to speak.

At age two years and nine months, it was obvious to us that there was something wrong. I took him to see Caroline, the GP, and she said she would make arrangements for us to see a speech therapist. We saw a lovely young speech therapist at the local clinic, and she said she would spend six weekly visits assessing him. After about four visits we received a letter from the clinic saying that due to funding problems the speech therapy service had been terminated. They would contact us again when it could be resumed. A few months went by, and Caroline wrote letters asking for therapy to be given in Dunstable. Eventually I drove him there, and another equally lovely young therapist started assessing him. After a couple of weeks another letter saying the service had been disbanded. In the end Caroline referred us to a paediatrician at the Royal Bucks hospital in Aylesbury. Along we went, and the consultant gave Freddie a thorough examination. His verdict was that 'Einstein didn't speak until he was four, so go away and stop worrying.'

Freddie by this time was older than three, and we thought attending the same nursery school as his sister, mornings only, might be just what was needed. By the time he was four we took him back to see the paediatrician at the hospital. His view was still 'Stop worrying', but he would arrange for Freddie to be assessed by the speech therapist at the hospital. Several times a month I would drive to Aylesbury, and we were given speech exercises for me to do with Freddie. I was told to continue at home with these, and to wait for the speech therapy services in Leighton Buzzard to resume. We felt we were getting nowhere, but we just didn't know where to turn. He still had no speech whatsoever, and the nursery school were very concerned.

When he turned six years old, and he could only say 'Mummy', I lost my temper and demanded to see the paediatrician again. He had stopped mentioning Einstein talking at four, and was all for passing us over to his speech therapist again. This time I was not going to be fobbed off, and I insisted we wanted the child to have a brain scan. His reply was, 'OK, but if there is anything on that scan, Mother, I will eat my hat.'

The scan was quite an ordeal for Freddie, but they managed to get what was needed. We waited quite a few weeks for the results, and then received an appointment for the paediatrician. It was with a very different attitude that he greeted us. The scan was so complicated that it had to be read by a professor in the north of England. It had shown damage to the speech area in Freddie's brain, which had shrunk more on one side than the other, and his skull had thickened round the outside to compensate. We were told how lots of work had been carried out in Northern Ireland on soldiers who had been shot in the head. They had shown how the brain forges new pathways around the damaged area, but very slowly. There was no eating of hats, and no kind of apology for us having to insist upon the scan. Instead we were told the scan hadn't taken us any further forward, and we must continue with speech therapy exercises.

I was in shock. I remember shaking all over as we drove home from Aylesbury. Our son was six years old and we had just been told he had brain damage. I had always imagined that if your baby had any kind of deformity, you knew when it was born. It was hard to take in what we had just been told. When we arrived home I can remember sitting on the bed and sobbing. I felt we were so alone, as if nobody cared, and we had no professional support, and nowhere to turn. The thoughts running through my head were, 'What is going to become of him? And what do we do?' I don't think I have ever felt so low as I did that day. I had a six-year-old child who could only say 'Mummy', and help was nowhere in sight.

2

Diagnosis

Gradually our family and close friends heard the news about Freddie's diagnosis, and I am sure they all had their feelings of upset and despair. They all tried to help, but there was nothing any of them could really do. Then my cousin's wife told me about an association she had read about. It was called AFASIC – short for Association For All Speech Impaired Children.

We contacted AFASIC and found there was a group in Bedfordshire. They held fairly regular meetings, and activities for the children, as well as having access to information from head office. It was as if someone had suddenly opened a door for us. The opportunity to meet with other parents who were facing the same problems was such a help, and a comfort. We were able to see how other families had dealt with non-existent speech therapy services, and inappropriate education. In the group we had a parent with a young daughter who had a massive speech problem. He just happened to be an educational psychologist by profession. He was great when it came to explaining all the legal procedures we had to go through to get our children special education. We had stepped into a previously unknown world overnight.

The most pressing problem we all needed to address was the lack of speech therapy services. The local education authority were saying it was the responsibility of the health service. The health service were saying they had no budget for it, and the education authority should provide. We threw ourselves into all the activities of the group.

During those early years of Freddie's life it was our practice to take a fortnight's holiday in the summer with our great friends Janice and Bryan, and their two children. Janice and I had met at school when we were seven years old, and remained good friends. Bryan had been best man at our wedding, and we kept in contact with them. They lived in Wiltshire, so we didn't see them as often as we would have liked. Our holidays together were precious, and we all looked forward to them. We would take a cottage or a bungalow in Cornwall, near the sea, and of course Rupert, our treasured golden retriever, would come too.

Annabelle and Tim, Janice and Bryan's younger son, would play together. Robin, their eldest, would look after Freddie, and showed amazing patience and care. We had so many laughs on those holidays; it was a tonic. Rupert's instinct to retrieve was very strong, and we were quite used to him sneaking into the bathroom to 'retrieve' whatever he could reach. The boys thought it was hilarious to find their mother's face cloth in the garden, or someone's slippers in the bath.

Rupert had the ability to cause chaos wherever he went. When young mothers would come to visit our house with their children, Rupert would like nothing more than striding around with a handbag in his mouth. He would carry bags by the strap and look very comical with a handbag − if you weren't the owner of the bag! He would mix up any possessions that unsuspecting visitors left lying around. To this day we have a cupboard in the hall we call 'The Ones Cupboard' because you could only ever find one of any pair of anything you had placed in the cupboard. We always said living with a golden retriever required a sense of humour, something my mother-in-law was not quick to display when Rupert deposited a whole stack of her snow-white, rather large knickers in a muddy puddle in the garden. She had stupidly unzipped the lid of her suitcase, which was on the floor. Rupert lifted the lid easily with his nose, and obviously selected the knickers. The milkman used to collect his money every Friday evening, and more often than not I would go to get my purse, and find the bag missing. The milkman would laugh heartily as I scoured the garden for it.

At age five Freddie had started full-time at the little school where he had attended the nursery. His sister had done the same thing, and he was able to stay there until he was seven. At age seven we sent him to the lower school along the road. The staff were all very perplexed by his lack of speech, and made the usual comments about how he should be receiving speech therapy.

A friend with a young lad who had serious dyslexia had taken him to London for a private assessment, as they wanted to know what extra help they could get for their son. This friend suggested we take Freddie. All we knew was what the brain scan had revealed, so it did seem to be a good idea. The assessment revealed that Freddie's IQ was very normal, and we found that highly encouraging.

The school called in their educational psychologist who came up with his findings, and his figures. He came to see me, and in a very polite way told me he thought Freddie should attend a local school for children with moderate learning difficulties. Freddie had to move on to another school at age nine, and the educational psychologist felt this would be the best course. I agreed to visit the school he suggested, and made an appointment to see the headmaster. When I walked in I knew immediately it wasn't right for Freddie. I showed the headmaster the assessment from the lady in London, and he said he didn't have one child in the school within 20 points of Freddie's IQ. He said his feeling was that Freddie needed a school specialising in speech and language.

I reported this conversation to the educational psychologist. who slapped me down with, 'You can get anyone to write anything if you pay them. The headmaster was only going on what you told him. That school in my opinion meets Freddie's needs.' Thank goodness for the AFASIC group, and the knowledge we had gained from the other parents. We knew we needed a document from the local education authority called a Statement of Special Needs. If this statement said they could meet your child's needs at a school in your county, then they didn't have to pay for the special speech and language school. There were only a handful of these specialist schools in the British Isles, so of course it meant the children had to board, and that came at a price.

I, like a lot of mothers, was filled with horror at the thought of my child, who couldn't speak many words, being sent away from the support of his family. By this time he was nearly nine, and decisions had to be made about his next school. I remember phoning the parent in AFASIC who was a professional educational psychologist in another county. He told me that if we could prove Freddie needed specialist speech and language therapy, and specialist schooling, I would have to come to terms with Freddie going to boarding school. I knew in my heart he was right, and I was going to have to face up to it, but I think it was a moment of realisation for me. I put the phone down and shook. I couldn't stop shaking, and John had to get me a stiff drink.

We wrestled with what we should do about Freddie's education. He wasn't particularly happy at school, and we knew he never had been. He was so isolated without speech. We felt the IQ number he had been given in London was right, and instinct told me the moderate learning difficulty school, however lovely, was not the place for him.

Annabelle, now nearly 12, was doing extremely well in a little school in Milton Keynes, so we approached them with our problem, and asked for advice. They suggested they should take Freddie for a year, and do a thorough assessment during that year. They would tell us the truth, and they made no promises about keeping him for more than a year. Again it was that word 'assessment'. It seemed Freddie spent his whole life being assessed by every Tom, Dick and Harry.

In the spring one of the children brought home a nasty sickness bug. As these things do, it swept through the household. Unfortunately we weren't on our own as a family. Janice and Bryan and their boys were staying. It started with one of our children, and then that night one of Janice and Bryan's boys dashed into their parents' room, waking them up by throwing up all over them and the bed. I think Annabelle was the next, and gradually we were all up. John can never forget standing in the garden in his pyjamas, hosing down carpet tiles at three o'clock in the morning.

It passed, and when we bid our guests farewell we joked we had celebrated better Easters. Everyone recovered, but I was slow to make improvement. I felt washed out, and low on energy. Freddie started his last term at the local school, and we were still worried about the next step for him. Our regular morning routine at that time was for another mum, who was a good friend, to drive Annabelle and her own children to the school in Milton Keynes. In the afternoon I would pick up Freddie from his school, and he would come with me in the car to Milton Keynes to bring all the children home.

21

This particular day, I was standing waiting at the entrance to Freddie's school. A friend informed me there were some photos of the children on display, just inside the front door. She suggested we walk down the path to have a look. I remember looking at the path to the door and saying to her, 'I just don't have the energy.' She looked at me, alarmed, and made a remark, quite kindly, about me still not being very well. I drove to Milton Keynes, picked up the children, minus Annabelle, who was going to tea with a friend. On the drive back I started to feel really exhausted. I kept telling myself, 'Just one more mile, one more mile.' I dropped my friend's children off at their house, and then goodness knows how I managed to make it home.

I opened the door, Freddie following, and staggered to a bed in the downstairs bedroom. I literally collapsed onto the bed, and I was so out of energy I couldn't speak. Freddie stood beside me, looking at me, just saying 'Mummy', and I couldn't do anything about it. I must have been lying on that bed for an hour, unable to move, and I was terrified. I couldn't understand what was happening. When John came in from work, I had managed to recover enough to speak, so he phoned the doctor's surgery and made me an appointment for the next day.

Fortunately Caroline was on duty at the surgery, and knew our family situation. She took some blood, and sent it away for testing, and advised me to rest. When you are a busy mum, rest doesn't come easily, but my friends were wonderful. Sarah did my share of the school runs, as well as her own, and Carole transported Freddie, and took him home with her children. It was early May, and the weather was quite warm. I spent most of the day just lying on a sunbed in the garden. Rupert was quite an old dog at 12, and he was happy to just plod round the garden and keep me company.

The blood tests came back and proved nothing. The weeks were passing and I wasn't getting any better. Caroline took more blood, tried antibiotics, and it just seemed to be a waiting game. More and more friends were helping with the children, and I felt quite distressed that I wasn't getting any better. One of my friends came round and told me how she knew of a similar situation with one of her cousins. The lady in question had even been into hospital, and they had taken small samples from her legs, but came up with nothing. She had finally been to see a doctor in Letchworth who was a conventionally trained doctor, but he also specialised in iridology (the study of the iris of the eye).

At that time I was desperate, if someone had told me to swing from a chandelier I would have done so. I made an appointment for the doctor in Letchworth. How I thought I was going to drive myself there and back from Leighton Buzzard, I don't know. I think I was so desperate for help that my thoughts were getting muddled. On the day of the appointment reality hit that I wasn't going to be able to drive. I phoned my next-door neighbour and wonderful friend, who always seems to be there for everyone in a crisis. She agreed to drive me to Letchworth, and not being a regular journey, long before the days of satellite navigation, we probably took a circuitous route, but we found the place. It was a small bungalow, and at first we weren't sure it was where we were meant to be.

I went in to see the doctor, a young dark-haired Belgian gentleman. He asked me lots of questions, studied my tongue, and had a good long look at my eyes through what I assumed to be a magnifying glass. He scribbled lots of notes, in very illegible writing, and then sat back in his chair.

He looked at me, and said, 'I am really sure this is myalgic encephalomyelitis, ME.' I must have stared at him. My brain was racing. I had seen a programme on the television about two sisters who had ME, and I had remarked to my husband what an awful illness it looked. At that time the newspapers were full of how fashionable it was to have ME, how City types were jumping on the bandwagon. They gave it the name 'Yuppy Flu', meaning that to get it you were young and an upwardly professional person.

All I could say was, 'Why do you think it is ME?'

He said, 'You are an absolutely classic case. It usually starts with a virus, there are all kinds of different trigger viruses, and the body's immune system doesn't seem to cope.'

He wrote out a sheet of instructions, which included what I should eat, and a list of dietary supplements. It had the word 'REST' written in large capital letters at the top of the page. Next appointment six weeks. I walked out to the dispenser lady at the front of the bungalow, and showed her my piece of paper. My head was in a whirl, 'ME?' I kept thinking. 'How has this happened to me, and what is all this writing that I can't read?' Fortunately the lady with all the supplement bottles and boxes knew what was required, and I paid my money and came away with a paper bag of strange pills and potions.

My neighbour was as taken aback as I was at the diagnosis. It was a first encounter with complementary medicine for both of us, and in 1988 it all seemed very strange. I remember walking into the little health food shop in Leighton Buzzard, and handing my doctor's sheet of notes to the owner of the shop. 'I don't know what I am going to live on,' I proclaimed. My instructions said I was to come off alcohol, caffeine, white flour, yeast and sugar. That meant sugar, as in anything that contains sugar, and so many foods do contain sugar. 'Don't worry,' he said, 'we all feel like that the first time.' He was wonderful, and filled a basket with an assortment of rice cakes, mung beans, herbal teas, and so on.

I have to say I felt very sceptical. I held all the supplements in my hand, and looked at my husband. 'What is all this rubbish I am supposed to take?'

His reply was, 'You have paid for it, don't waste it now by throwing it in the bin. You have nothing else to try, you must at least try it.'

Those early days were hard. I felt as if my whole life had been thrown in the air, and had come crumbling down around me. I felt indescribably awful, and exhausted. I could no longer run the house and look after the children, and to cap it all I couldn't eat and drink the things I had known all my life. I felt I had to get to grips with making wholemeal scones, without the energy to do it, so that I didn't starve to death.

I decided to take the supplements and try my hardest with the diet so that I could prove to myself, and everyone else, that this was nonsense. My next appointment with Caroline, the GP, came round and I sat in the waiting room wondering what the latest tests would reveal. The patient before me came out, and it seemed I sat for a long time before Caroline called me in. It flashed through my thoughts that she was trying to find a way to break the news to me that it was ME. As it happened, that was exactly the case.

Her words to me were, 'Wendy, I don't know how to tell you this, but I think it is ME.' I instantly put her out of her misery by telling her I had already been told that by a complementary doctor in Letchworth. She was very interested in all his suggestions, and the list of supplements. She said, with a very puzzled expression, 'I have no idea what these are, but I can say they don't look like anything that will do you harm. I have nothing I can give you. I think it is ME, and I am sure all the stress and worry you have had with Freddie's problems have played a large part in this. Your immune system has just become very low. If you want to try pushing and pulling your diet, and trying this new regime, that is fine by me. I just want to keep an eye on you, and see none of this causes harm.' I thought this was fair comment, and left, wondering how long it would take for me to recover.

Earlier in the year we had booked a special treat of a holiday. The children were older now at 12 and 9, and Janice and Bryan had decided to take their boys camping in France. We decided to book a self-catering villa in Majorca for a week in July. Rupert was a very old dog, so my in-laws had agreed to come and dog-sit. The bill for the final payment dropped through the letter box. We had to make the decision to cancel. There was no way I could walk to the check-in desk at the airport, let alone anything else. Everyone was disappointed and I felt I had let everyone down. The school holidays arrived, and the next headache of how to amuse the children. I wasn't any better, but I wasn't any worse. Friends were still being wonderful, taking the children off my hands.

Freddie left the local lower school, and we thanked all the teachers and said our 'goodbyes'. I remember feeling very sad the day he left, as we were taking the next step along Freddie's pathway with no idea whether we were doing the right thing. We had decided the year of assessment at the school in Milton Keynes was the safest option. That meant change for Freddie again, and I felt very sorry for him with his lack of speech and understanding of language. He had gained a few more words in his vocabulary, but he hadn't yet mastered joining them into sentences.

My next appointment at Letchworth came round, and another selection of supplements. I was still not convinced, but as my husband had pointed out, I had no other avenues to explore. Gradually, and very slowly, I started to get a little more energy.

September brought the new school term, and we were still relying very heavily on friends. By October I was definitely showing small signs of recovery, so to make up to the children for the cancellation of the family holiday in July, we decided to try to book anything we could, in this country, for their half-term holiday. I sent John to the travel agents one wet and miserable Saturday, with the instruction, 'Just get anything.'

When he returned he said, 'Well you did say get anything, and there was no choice.' It was one week's full board at a holiday camp in Skegness. My face must have been a study; it wasn't quite what I had expected, but the kids would probably love it.

Our good friends and neighbours all laughed when they heard our plans. They all knew we loved the quiet little coves and moors of Cornwall, and this was going to be different. The in-laws came to dog-sit, and we set off for Skegness. The chalet we were allocated was due for demolition the following week, but I had a bed to lie on, and the children loved the activities. The weather was good for the time of year, and the chalet being very near the beach meant I could walk slowly down to the sands. I enjoyed the sea air, and just sitting looking at the sea, even if I was wrapped in a blanket.

Freddie loved the monorail train, and with Annabelle looking after him they were able to ride around quite frequently. The food was put in front of us, so I didn't have to cook, and although it wasn't fine dining, it was perfectly acceptable, and good value for what we paid. I had taken a bag of rice cakes, fresh fruit, and so on for myself, so as long as they supplied vegetables, I could exist.

Meals were taken in the big dining hall, and Annabelle was most amused at the practice of people having to stand on their chairs if it was their birthday. Everyone would clap very loudly as a birthday cake was brought in, complete with lots of bright candles. We teased her that we would say it was her birthday, and she would have to stand on her chair. The thought nearly made her hide under the table.

Another highlight of the week was the 'Crush a Grape Show' at the theatre. Being children's entertainment it was packed, and we all took our seats in the middle of a row. I was next to Freddie, and the show started with bangs, and fireworks, and flashing lights. Obviously Freddie hadn't been expecting that, and in his fright managed to projectile vomit all over the seat in front. By some miracle the occupant of the seat had just left for some reason, but in the dark I had to skirmish around with handkerchiefs trying to clear up the mess. Annabelle and John were so embarrassed they pretended they weren't with us, and my pleas for help from them were met with stony stares straight ahead. I had to escort Freddie all along the rest of the row, and out of the theatre, just hoping he wouldn't do it again.

When we were outside I could see the funny side. I started to laugh, and Freddie looked at me and said 'Why laugh, Mummy?' It was probably the first time I had laughed since May when the ME began, and I think that was when I started to improve, thanks to my supplements.

On our return from Skegness we tried to get back into a routine again, and I would rest for most of the morning, then try to drive to Milton Keynes in the afternoon to collect the children from school. The other mum I shared the driving with was 'on call', just in case I didn't have the strength. Rupert was now very slow on his feet, and looking a poor old chap. He slept most of the day, but he did still like to think he had been for a walk. We would try to walk a few yards down the road and back again. It suited both of us nicely. 'Poor old things together', I used to say to him.

The local newspaper in Leighton Buzzard has always dropped through our letter box on Tuesdays. Just browsing through it I came across an article, written by a couple living in the town, who both had ME. They had been interviewed by the paper, and were talking about their experience of coping with ME together. They were thinking of starting a support group in the town, and were asking other sufferers to get in touch. I immediately phoned them, and they asked me to go to a meeting they were going to hold in a local hall. It was surprising how many people turned up. Some were carers, who had come on behalf of their sons or daughters, and it was decided with the help of carers perhaps we could form a group to hold regular meetings. Also, if we had enough family members who would volunteer, to raise funds for ME research.

I found it a great help talking to other people about their situation with the illness, and hearing what remedies had helped in any way. It was also quite frightening to meet so many young people, more girls than boys, who were so seriously affected that they hardly left their homes. Nobody had a magic cure, but it was apparent that the complementary pathway I was taking had worked for one other lady. Looking back now as I write this, I am still in touch with quite a few of the members of that original group. Sadly, some of the young girls are still very housebound after 25 years.

We had speakers for the meetings, something like a demonstration of kinesiology. The night the kinesiologist came I was the guinea pig on the couch. The demonstration was given by a charming, quietly-spoken elderly gentleman. He showed how he did the muscle testing by lifting my arm. He pushed against my hand very gently and I had to resist. He assessed the strength in the muscles, and then addressed a question to my body as he put his other hand on various areas of my head.

According to the reaction he received from the muscle, he seemed to know whether there was a problem. For example, if his other hand was gently pressing on the thyroid area, he would ask if there was a problem there. When he received a response from the arm muscle he was testing and he thought there was a problem, he proceeded to carry out what he called a 'correction'. He would close his eyes and remain standing with his hand on the affected area until he yawned. He explained that was his own personal way of working and when he yawned he knew the correction was complete.

It was all very baffling and alien to most of us, especially when he attempted to diagnose our chairman, who was the father of an ME sufferer. He asked him to stand beside me with his hand on my shoulder. By testing my muscles and asking a question about the chairman, the kinesiologist was able to diagnose a complaint for the chairman. It just didn't seem possible to us, but the chairman had to admit it was absolutely correct.

When the kinesiologist left we all had our own little discussion about what we had seen. Some were very sceptical, and there was quite a bit of giggling, but the fact remained that the diagnosis of the chairman's complaint was correct. Someone suggested it was a form of spiritual healing, and that was the only explanation offered. It was an interesting and thought-provoking meeting.

On another occasion we had a demonstration of dowsing. The dowser showed us how the dowsing rods moved over the water pipes in the floor of the hall. We all then took turns in trying to do the same thing. It was amazing how the rods swung for all of us, and we knew we weren't moving them ourselves.

At a later date the dowser and his wife came to Leighton Buzzard, and dowsed for geopathic stress around the homes of any of the group who wanted it done. Geopathic stress is caused by underground water. I am told in Germany they dowse for geopathic stress before they build new houses. He found quite bad energy lines in a number of our houses and gardens, and pegged them for us.

The meetings ran, on and off, for a while, but in the end it became obvious that we didn't get enough people to make them viable, as everyone was too ill. We did have a good try at the fund raising with the help of family and friends. For a while we had market stalls at the May Day Fayre in the town, or the Carnival, and any local event. After that we did the street collections outside the supermarket, or in the High Street.

To make it easier, and more fun to recruit volunteers, we negotiated a reduced rate on fancy dress outfits from the hire shop. The lady who ran the shop was very kind to us, and people were far keener to stand in the street holding a tin if they were in disguise. I can remember being Mr Blobby, and we also had Sylvester the Cat, and the Pink Panther. It was very hot inside the masks, especially if they were rubbery. Parents would give in to pester power from their children, and we collected a lot of money from children who looked at Sylvester the Cat with an amazed expression on their faces. It was also quite interesting when people you knew came along and hadn't a clue who was in the crazy outfit. People you had previously regarded as being very generous wouldn't come anywhere near, and the old guy down the road you had always thought of as Scrooge would put an amazing amount in the tin!

The group dwindled, people moved away, and people weren't well enough to fund-raise. It ended up with four or five of us meeting in the supermarket coffee shop now and again. We would laugh a lot at ourselves, and the ridiculous situations the illness created. In fact we made so much noise we became

31

known to the lady who regularly served us as 'the rowdies'. After a few years the supermarket expanded, and the coffee shop closed to house the internet shopping section. I am still in touch with some of the members of the old group, and we still try to support one another as much as we can.

3

East Croydon Station

I continued to make visits to the doctor in Letchworth. They would be at something like two-monthly intervals. Each time, after a detailed inspection of my eyes, the doctor would say, 'This time we are going to aim some ammunition at your liver', or whatever organ it was that needed help. I would come away with my handwritten instruction sheet, and some of the supplements would be discontinued, and new ones inserted in the list. As I was gaining more strength and energy, I believed more in what I was taking. The doctor spent time explaining the changes to the supplements, and why we were making them. The object was to give the body as much help as possible, and not hinder it – hence the no sugar, no alcohol or caffeine regime. I was well enough to drive myself to Letchworth each time, and I became more and more committed to the treatment.

The GP was very pleased with my progress, and said I was certainly not taking anything harmful. She was happy to see me doing so well, when she knew she couldn't help me. I reached a stage where the complementary medicine doctor decided to drop the regular visits, and just kept me on a basic list of supplements. He had taught me how to listen to my body, and I could phone him if I needed. He was still there for me.

Freddie was in his second term at the school in Milton

Keynes, and I was trying not to think too far ahead about the verdict on his future schooling. We were ticking along, but emotional upset was just around the corner.

Dear old Rupert, my big teddy bear of a dog, was getting slower by the day. Walks were no longer on the agenda, and he just plodded in and out of the house to the garden. His coat was looking ragged, and his eyes were glassy. It was a Saturday morning when I came down to find he couldn't stand on his legs. He was just slumped on the kitchen floor. He gave me such an imploring look, I knew he was in pain. I phoned the vet and asked her to come to the house.

It was a terrible wait that morning. I sat with him as much as I could. I told the children they must prepare themselves for the worst. My husband was so upset that he busied himself with other things, and, unlike me, he couldn't sit with Rupert.

Two lovely ladies arrived about midday, the vet and her assistant. She examined Rupert and said his kidneys had failed. She explained she couldn't treat him any further, and the kindest thing was to put him gently to sleep. My husband took the children to another part of the house. I told the vet I wanted to stay with him. I loved him so much, I wasn't going anywhere in his hour of need. I watched as the anaesthetic was put into the vein in his paw, and his head lowered. The vet listened for a heartbeat and then told me he had gone. She was so kind, and professional, but I know it affects the vets as well as the owners. I patted and stroked him, and then when I was convinced he had gone, I left the room and let the vets take the body away. I went to join the others, and we all stood in a huddle crying. We said to one another, 'He is out of his pain now', trying to comfort each other. Freddie, however, was not displaying the emotion I expected, and just said, 'More room in house.' We ignored him, and set about putting Rupert's big wicker basket, with its chewed sides, and all his leads, bowls and blankets, into the loft. I couldn't bear to part with them, but we had to put them out of sight.

I went next door to tell my good friend Louise what had happened, and we both wept all over her kitchen floor. John did his crying walking round the garden, and I don't know how we passed the rest of the day. Bedtime was awful. I was lying in bed just sobbing silent sobs. I thought my heart would explode, and I was overwhelmed with the grief.

As I lay there I suddenly had a strange experience. I caught just a glimpse of a waggy tail in the darkness. It didn't really register with me what I had seen until the next day. It was very odd. I knew it wasn't a dream, but what was it? It wasn't Rupert's shaggy old tail. Halfway through the morning I felt motivated to look at the old photograph albums. I wasn't sure whether it was a wise move, but I somehow felt compelled to do it. I looked back over the baby photos, and then I saw it. It was a photo of Rupert as a young dog, and there was his young beautiful tail. That was what I had glimpsed, and I had forgotten it looked like that when he was young. I can't explain this at all. I am not a medium, and although I would love to develop psychic abilities, they never seem to come. It should have been a comfort to me, but my grief was so raw, nothing was a comfort.

Prior to losing Rupert, on our return from the holiday camp in Skegness, we had talked about what we should, or should not, book for our holiday the following year. We decided that as I had weathered the week in Skegness, surely by August I would be well enough for Center Parcs. I hadn't liked leaving Rupert in the house with the in-laws, so we booked one of the lodges at the Sherwood Forest resort that took dogs. Losing Rupert in the April was a blow, and seeing all the other dog owners with their dogs in August was very sad. It brought home to us that Rupert was on the booking form, and he wasn't there with us. We didn't feel ready for another dog, there were so many uncertainties in our life. My health was one factor, and the other was Freddie's education.

At the end of the school year we had been invited to a meeting with the head of the Milton Keynes school to discuss their findings. They felt strongly that the right place for Freddie was a specialist speech and language school. Like us, they thought the IQ assessment in London was correct. Freddie had missed so much learning because of his lack of understanding of speech, and they felt he needed the specialist speech therapy that was only available in such schools. We couldn't argue with any of this. We had been saying exactly the same things to the education authority, but what we said was just dismissed.

The school explained they were prepared to help us in applying for the formal document called the Statement of Special Educational Needs. They said we were to write a formal letter to the education authority saying we were going to commence proceedings through the court, and Freddie's present school were going to be our professional witnesses. Being a non-state school they could do this for us, as they were independent. They suggested we research the specialist schools in the country, and decide which one we wanted Freddie to attend. We were then to press for this school. In the meantime they would keep Freddie.

We came away with mixed feelings. On the one hand we knew what they were saying was right, but it meant, for me, that I would have to face up to the fact Freddie would be going away to boarding school. Also a legal battle could ensue, and we would have to go to court with all that entailed. I wasn't sure I had the appetite for it, still being in the grips of ME, and only functioning on my dietary supplements, and high dosed vitamin and mineral pills.

AFASIC came into its own with advice about schools, and we decided to visit a specialist school near Oxted in Surrey. The day of the appointment, John took time off work, and with heavy hearts we made our way round the M25. When we arrived we walked through the door into a world we didn't know existed. There were all these little Freddies! They were just like him. The atmosphere was happy, and the staff so caring. We were shown into the speech therapy department. 'Department?' I thought, as I looked at all the different rooms, with different names of the therapists on the doors. We couldn't track down one for any length of time in Bedfordshire, and here they were, rows of them in one place! By this time we were just filled with amazement. We couldn't believe all this had existed and we hadn't been aware.

We met the headmaster, and went into his office for a chat. The headmaster asked us about Freddie, and as we stumbled to explain he finished our sentences for us with a smile. Here was a man who actually knew what we were talking about, and what we coped with. It was the first time in Freddie's life that we felt we had been fully understood, and Freddie's problems correctly identified. We came away knowing this was where Freddie needed to be, and I felt a lot more reassured about the whole thing.

Our next step was to report back to Freddie's school in Milton Keynes on our findings. They said they would tell the education authority that they could not meet Freddie's needs – in other words, they were throwing him out – and they would back us in our application to the court. We told the authority we wanted Freddie to attend the school in Surrey, and we were prepared to take legal action if necessary.

It wasn't a short process, but the local education authority agreed to pay for Freddie to be assessed at the Surrey school. It was a two-day assessment, and by an amazing coincidence one of my colleagues, from the days when I worked in London, lived opposite the school. She looked out across the village green right at the school. We stayed with her and her family, which was a wonderful support for me. It must have been a bewildering experience for a little lad who understood so little of the world, but at least he didn't have to stay the night in the school.

The school assessed him as being entirely suitable for a place, and wrote to the local education authority accordingly. We thought it would all be sorted out within the year, but the legal machinery just ground on. Although we didn't have to go to court, it took another two years of Freddie's life before he started at the new school. By this time he was 12 years old, he had been at the school in Milton Keynes for three years, and he still couldn't put words into sentences.

When the day came to take him to the school with all his luggage I had at least been thinking about it for some time, and had become more familiar with the idea. I had spent hours sewing name tapes into socks, underwear and pyjamas, as well as his uniform. I stitched his name on his face cloth, and carved his initials in his soap! I had talked endlessly to Freddie about staying at school overnight, and how he could come home at weekends.

Surprisingly friends and relatives hadn't been too supportive. Many people told us we were being, cruel, selfish, and we would break his heart. Thank goodness for the other mothers and fathers in AFASIC who knew what a wrench it was, and how hard it was for us to hand him over at the school, and come home.

I will never forget Freddie standing in a classroom looking at us in disbelief, saying 'I feel sick.' The teacher replied, 'Don't we all, dear', and waved us out of the door.

It soon became obvious that Freddie had settled, and for the first time in his life he was in a school where he didn't feel the odd one out. He wasn't different from everyone else, they were all like him. They all went for their speech therapy sessions, it was the norm. I knew he had settled the day I spoke to him on the phone, and he said, 'No come home weekend', which meant, 'Do I *have* to come home at the weekend?'

We soon got to know the other parents who lived in Buckinghamshire, and we started to share the journeys backwards and forwards at the weekends as much as possible. One very helpful father always picked them up in his car on a Friday afternoon. He worked in London and finished on a Friday lunchtime. We took our turn on the M25 on alternate Sunday afternoons, and we considered ourselves very lucky to have such help from the others.

It was on bank holidays that the journey became tricky because of the extra traffic on the M25, so on these occasions I would volunteer to use my railcard, and take all the children back on the train. There was one journey that will remain in my memory for ever. Because the most obvious route by train involved crossing London, I opted to drive the children to the village of Harlington, where we could catch a Thameslink train. That meant we didn't have to cross London.

It was only 20 minutes in the car, and the parents dropped the children off at our house. It was a fairly hot sunny day, the car journey was fine, and we caught our train at Harlington. We hadn't travelled more than a couple of stations, when Liam's finger started to pour with blood. What he had cut it on I never did find out, but thankfully the man with the sandwich trolley was passing through our carriage at the time. He, dear man, whisked out a first aid kit, and soon had Liam patched up with a neat plaster.

Drama over, I decided it was time to produce the cakes I had in my bag. Tracey, a fairly plump eleven-year-old, with no recognisable speech at all, was delighted to get her hands on the cakes. Before I could distribute them round, she grabbed as many as possible, and started throwing them round the carriage at the other passengers. I was horrified, I didn't know where to turn first, whether to pick up the cakes, tell her off, or apologise to people. The others brightened and saw signs of a good game shaping up. I felt very embarrassed, especially as people who didn't know the situation must have thought the children were out of control, and making very strange noises. I calmed them down, and started to count the number of stations left.

The train was just slowing down on the approach to East Croydon station, where we had to change trains on to the line that went to Oxted. Mark, a small ten-year-old, with a few physical disabilities, needed the toilet urgently. As well as no clear speech, he had a big personality, sometimes bordering on distinctly stroppy. I knew he had a problem in the toilet direction, and when he needed the loo he needed it quickly. He was all for dashing off to the toilet on the train, but I couldn't let him go, or we would fail to get off the train at East Croydon. I promised him we would go straight to the disabled toilet on the platform. I managed to get all four of them off the train, with Mark holding himself and protesting loudly. We hurried along to the toilets, and there was the 'Out of Order' notice. 'Please use toilets on the other platform.' I explained to Mark, and hurried everyone, together with their assorted bags, over the bridge and down onto the platform. Fortunately I knew the loos were in the waiting room. The waiting room had automatic glass sliding doors, quite modern for its time, and was in the middle of two platforms. There were rows of seats either side, the doors were in the middle on both sides, and the toilets were in the far corner. Poor Mark was going nearly blue in the face by this time, and I raced the children to the doors.

The doors were stuck, no way would they open. The people inside sat on their seats just staring at us, looking like goldfish in a bowl. I saw the doors on the opposite side open, so I made the children run up the platform, and sat them all on a seat, bar Mark. 'Sit there, don't move, and do not get on any train,' I said sternly. 'Freddie, you see that nobody gets on a train, even if it is our train. You all sit there while I take Mark to the loo.'

I raced Mark all round the outside of the waiting room and in through the working doors. We ran to the Ladies, as I couldn't let him in the Gents on his own. When we opened the door, horror of horrors, there was a queue of ladies. I was desperate, let alone Mark, so in a very flustered voice I addressed the queue. 'Please,' I said, 'can you let this little disabled lad have the next available cubicle, he really is so desperate he will have an accident any minute.' They all looked at me, weighing me up, and I could feel them thinking 'Who is this mad woman?' A door opened, and I dashed forward with Mark. The ladies all stood staring, I bundled him into the loo, and then stood outside holding the door just a fraction open, so that he couldn't lock himself in. If he locked it I thought, with his lack of dexterity, he would never get it open.

No sooner had I managed to get him in there than the loudspeaker system announced a train, and I could hear it thunder in on the platform we needed. I had a picture in my head of Liam, Tracey and Freddie getting on the train. I knew I had to check them. I turned to the nearest lady in the queue and said, 'Please can you just put your foot in this door for me and make sure he doesn't lock the door. I have three more disabled children I have left sitting on the platform, and I can't risk them getting on this train.'

I dashed out into the waiting room, straight to the doors, and they wouldn't open, so it had to be the others, and run all the way round. More hard stares from the zombies sitting in the waiting room. I ran round the end of the building, and what a relief, they were still sitting there.

'Train,' protested Freddie, pointing anxiously.

'I know,' I said, 'but you must not get on it, any of you. Mark is still in the loo. I will go and get him, but promise me you won't get on the train.'

I gave the non-opening doors another go, but still I had to do my marathon run right round the building to the doors the other side. You would have thought at least one of the passengers in the waiting room would have grinned as I raced towards the loos, but there was no sign of the lady I left with her foot in the door. Instead Mark was still in the loo, and, more horrors, he had locked the door!

I didn't know whether to laugh or cry, but just went into sensible mode. I spoke to Mark through the door as calmly as I could. I really wanted to shout a couple of swear words asking him why he had locked the door, but instead I talked him through sliding the bolt along. Someone must have been helping me that day, because the door opened. I took him by the hand, saying, 'Don't worry about washing your hands, I have some wet wipes in my bag. We don't have the time.' I didn't even bother with the non-opening doors, we just ran the circuit round the building one more time. The guard was on the platform checking the doors of the train, and saw me coming. I gathered up the three on the seat, who were quite agitated by this time. The guard waited patiently as I herded them into a carriage. I slumped into my seat thinking 'Never again.' As the train pulled out of the platform I had one last glance at the waiting room. Still the same faces were staring, but this time, would you believe it, the faulty doors were opening wide to let somebody through.

The rest of the journey seemed to go quite quickly as I tried to get my breath back. We eventually drew into Hurst Green station, and we set off across the village green towards the school. I was thinking to myself, 'What a journey!' The distant sounds of an emergency vehicle could be heard. We kept walking towards the school, and the siren seemed to be getting louder. Then there was the faint sound of a fire alarm. As we neared the school I could see groups of people standing around. The fire engine came roaring along, and in through the school gates. A little voice in my head was saying, 'Please don't tell me I have to take them all home.'

I spotted Freddie's house-mother with a small group of children. 'Don't worry,' she said, 'it's nothing serious, I think someone burnt the toast in the staff room, and if the alarm goes off it is automatically linked to the fire station.'

I gathered the children in her direction and said, 'They are all yours. I have had a pig of a journey, and I must dash to catch my train home.'

I walked back across the village green, and I think I could have cheered when my train drew in, and I was on my way home, alone!

4

The Code

It was the beginning of a new era when Freddie started at the boarding school. Weekends revolved around the journeys on the M25, but Freddie stayed at school at the weekend more and more, depending on what activities he didn't want to miss. I was hoping for more peace during the week, now that I was free from constant paperwork and lobbying for speech therapy. When Freddie finally left the school in Milton Keynes, Annabelle was reaching sixth form stage. We decided that she seemed to be heading for university, but we were concerned that she had led a very sheltered school life. It was a tough decision, but we decided to send her to the local upper school for sixth form. Looking back it was probably not one of our better ideas.

Annabelle was quite happy at the thought of changing school. A lot of her friends were also leaving, and I think she had become rather bored with the same old routines. At 16 her thoughts were on her social life, and a new school and new friends sounded like more fun. As parents we had talked to her about her future, what options she had for her A level subjects, university, and the serious stuff parents are concerned about.

Another new girl joined the school, and the same class, when Annabelle started. She had moved into the area so she was another new face alongside Annabelle. The two of them became good friends and I was pleased it had happened on day one. The boys in their class had been used to the same familiar female faces around them and were quite taken with the two new girls in their midst!

Schoolwork became the last thing on Annabelle's mind. After only a couple of weeks she started treating us to teenage door slamming, and the constant arguments about everything. I would drop her off at the school in the morning, and she made her own way home in the afternoon. I didn't see an awful lot of studying going on at home, but I thought all was well. It was only when I was emptying her waste-paper bin that I wondered why weekday train tickets to Milton Keynes came tumbling out. I looked at the dates and phoned the school to check she had been there on those days. There was a lot of 'Well, once they are over sixteen they don't have to attend school if they don't want to,' and I had to prod them hard to find out that their registers were very sketchy.

It looked highly likely that she had been bunking off and we made it clear it had to stop. We were beginning to worry that we had made a very bad decision and reminded ourselves that most teenagers go through a bad rebellious phase. Also, it was better it was happening now, while she was at home. At the end of the year the only glowing report she had was from the sports teacher. Annabelle would admit she has never been a girl to enjoy sport. She was far more into arts and crafts, so it was very surprising to us when she came home with a marvellous report from the sports teacher. We read it, and re-read it, and thought there must have been a mix-up with the names. When we questioned her she told us she always marked the register for the teacher because he didn't know the names of the pupils. He had given her a good report as thanks for her help.

At the end of her first year at sixth form my cousin phoned to ask if Annabelle would like to spend a weekend with her daughters, Emma and Rebekah. Emma was in her first year at university, and having a great time. She wanted her younger sister to stay for the weekend, and wondered if Annabelle would like to join them. It turned out to be just what we needed. Emma gave them a super weekend, Annabelle enjoyed every minute of it, and instantly thought, 'I like the look of this party lifestyle, this is for me.' Realising that if she wanted to join Emma at university she had to get herself some A levels, she started to do some work. She wouldn't apply for any other university, just Emma's, and she wanted to read the same subject.

During this time I was still taking my high-dose vitamin and mineral pills, which I saw as my 'go pills'. I had learnt that pacing myself was everything. If I picked up an infection of any kind, or a virus, it was instantly back to the ME symptoms, and I had to rest to throw it off.

I had a good friend who had a beautifully behaved golden retriever bitch, and I knew she wanted to breed from her. I discussed it with John, and we said how nice it would be to have one of Ellie's puppies. When I met Pauline, and she said Ellie was definitely having a litter of puppies, we decided the opportunity was too good to miss. We knew we could never replace our dear old Rupert, so we would have a bitch. We named her Poppy, and she was a dainty little bundle of light cream fluff when she joined the family.

She became my constant companion and followed me from room to room. She decided she was my dog, and she never really had any time for anyone else. It was quite embarrassing that when John came home from a day's work, instead of greeting him with doggy wild ecstasy, she would walk past him without so much as a wag of the tail. She was very well

47

behaved, and made no secret of the fact she adored me, and nobody else mattered!

She certainly demonstrated her feelings the day we were strolling through a small area of woodland. It was a popular place for local dog walkers, and Poppy and I quite often took the route through the woods on our daily walk. We were walking along when suddenly a young man in dark clothing stepped out from behind a tree. It made both Poppy and me jump with surprise, and I really don't know whether he was an innocent lad taking a short cut through the woods, or whether he had any ill intent. Poppy wasn't taking any chances. She pinned the guy against a tree, showing him her full set of beautiful white teeth. I put her on a short lead, and apologised to the lad, explaining she was very protective of me. If he did have any ill intent, he certainly wasn't going to take any chances while I had her around. If he was innocent, he was obviously relieved I had her under control. I always felt safe with her around me after that.

In late September 1993, shortly before her eighteenth birthday, Annabelle joined Emma at university. She settled well, and we were relieved that the rocky days of sixth form were over. It should have been a quiet, blissful time for us in Leighton Buzzard, with both the children away from home in term-time.

Freddie's speech was finally coming along at a steady pace, he was happier at school than he had ever been, and we were feeling confident we had made the right decisions. The trouble was, it was time to start thinking where he should go, and what he should do, when he reached age 16. The school he was attending had no sixth form, so we were once again taking advice from AFASIC and the other parents we knew. The speech therapists were strongly in favour of him moving on to a place where he could continue with his speech therapy, as he had missed out so much in his early years.

We started to visit colleges, and then a similar specialist school in Derbyshire, that did take them until age 18. We were very impressed with the school, so it was back to applying to the local education authority, and getting stuck into endless paperwork again. Fortunately Freddie's present school were very supportive of our decision, and choice of school, so this time we didn't have to consider the possibility of legal action. I labelled new clothing, and gave up on carving initials into soap. The soap always returned at the end of term still neatly initialled, together with the face cloth bearing its carefully ironed creases!

In September 1995 Freddie started at the new school, and it made a change to be using the M1 instead of the M25. Freddie took to it straight away. He was staying in a large house in the centre of Matlock – next door to the police station, so no worries there! There were several students living in the house, assisted by their key workers. They caught the regular bus service to the school, which was located in a village a few miles outside Matlock. For Freddie it was school three days a week, Chesterfield college one day, and the school's own work experience centre in Derby on the fifth day. There was a very good speech therapy unit at the school, and the therapists also worked alongside the students in class.

Freddie settled in well to the new life. The house in Matlock gave the students a certain amount of freedom. Freddie had good friends for playing snooker, or a group of them would go to a leisure centre to play badminton. At weekends they could watch a local football match if they wanted, usually to cheer on Freddie's key worker! They had to take turns with the chores, such as cooking, washing up, and doing their own washing and ironing. They even went out some evenings with a key worker 'bat watching'.

The work experience centre took the form of a garden centre with a café, chicken house and woodwork unit. The students all took turns in trying out the different jobs, and selecting their favourites to explore further. Freddie definitely favoured the retail side, so his key worker secured him a Sunday job for eight Sundays, working in a supermarket in Matlock. We had never seen Freddie so happy as he was in those days.

We, as parents, had regular meetings with the staff at the end of term. It was at one of these meetings with Freddie's speech therapist, that we first learnt he had Asperger's syndrome, which to use the technical term, is on the autistic spectrum. Not only did he have the Asperger's, but also a high-level speech and language disorder, with emphasis on the receptive language – in other words, difficulty understanding language. We talked about Freddie's brain scan at six years old, and for the first time someone suggested the brain damage could have been caused by the high temperature, and fever, I had with the mumps. I still find it incredible to believe that it took us so many years before we were given chapter and verse about Freddie's disability.

As the end of Freddie's two years at Matlock approached, we had to start thinking in terms of what was going to happen when he returned home. The school made it very clear that we were not on our own with this process. They wanted to be fully involved, and gave us very good support. A special needs careers lady in Bedfordshire visited the school in Derbyshire, and spent time talking to Freddie about his preferences for work. She set up a meeting with an organisation called the Training Agency, which was part of Dunstable College, a few miles from Leighton Buzzard. It was agreed that Freddie would attend at Dunstable for assessment, and they would try to find him a work placement on a government-supported employment scheme. He would attend the Training Agency one day a week. Freddie's key worker was keen to see this all worked out, and if there were any problems he would visit Dunstable to try to smooth the pathway. We couldn't have praised the school enough for their support at that time.

It was a hot sunny July in 1997 when Freddie finally left Matlock, and for two weeks a group of them went on a National Trust working holiday in the Lake District. He had terrific fun those two weeks, and it was a wonderful idea on the school's part to organise it as a finale to their school days.

Annabelle by this time had acquired her degree, a job in human resources, and was in a serious relationship. Very shortly after finishing university she moved out from home and moved in with her boyfriend. This meant that when Freddie came back from boarding school we were now three and a dog.

It was a novelty for Freddie to be back home again, and he was glad to be settled into his own bedroom. The downside of being away was that he came home to no local friends. Living in the house in Matlock, there was always someone who would have a game of darts. The house was always full of fun, there was plenty to do, and lots of company. He joined in with us with whatever we were doing, but that summer was one of adjustment.

In September he started going to Dunstable to the Training Agency. They asked him what line of work he wanted, and he told them he would like to work in a supermarket or a garden centre. He had sampled both in Derbyshire. It wasn't long before they took him for an interview at a supermarket in Leighton Buzzard. The supermarket had applied for someone on the supported employment programme. He would be paid a small amount of money, but he would be supported and supervised by the Bedfordshire training programme.

We were delighted, to say the least, when he was given the place. It was a full-time job, five days a week. He started work in early November, and to begin with he had one day a week at the Training Agency in Dunstable. After all the years of worrying − would he ever speak? would we get him to the right schools? and whatever would he do in life? − he had a job. OK maybe not a straightforward employment situation, but he was occupied, and learning skills. We were euphoric.

In life, euphoria never seems to last long. Bad news came in the form of a phone call from my sister, Sue. She lived in a village just outside Lymington, so visited our parents very regularly. 'Mum is really poorly,' she said, 'and Dad isn't coping well.'

I knew something had been going on with my mother's health. Mum and Dad loved their coach trips. They were both 81, and they liked the company of the other elderly folk, together with the security of being looked after, and organised, by the coach drivers. They had done so many coach holidays with the same company that they knew all the drivers. It was part of the excitement at the beginning of the trip to see which driver it was. In July they had been to Jersey, and whilst there, Mum hadn't seemed too well. In September it was Scotland, and in Carlisle Mum had sudden chest pain and was admitted to hospital. The first thing the hospital did was take a blood sample, and it was discovered that Mum had previously suffered a heart attack. When questioned she had said, 'Yes I know, it happened in Jersey, but I didn't want to spoil the holiday.' I think Mum received a ticking off from the Sister on the ward, and she was monitored for a few days, and given medication for her heart.

The coach obviously had to move on to Scotland, so Mum was in hospital, and Dad in a hotel. The problem was how to get them back to Hampshire when Mum was refusing to travel by road. Dad wanted to hire an Air Ambulance, and Mum was refusing that as nonsense. In the end we hatched a plan whereby I contacted Carlisle and Milton Keynes stations to arrange for wheelchair assistance at either end of the journey by train. We met the train in Milton Keynes and brought them to Leighton Buzzard for the night. Sue and her husband volunteered to drive up and take them back to Lymington by car. Mum and Dad settled for this compromise, but it didn't turn out to be ideal, as their pre-booked train seats were in a carriage with a party of noisy school children!

Once safely back in Lymington, Mum didn't seem to become her old self. There were two further visits to the local hospital, for draining fluid away from her chest cavity. It wasn't clear what the problem was; or if it was clear to the doctors, nothing was being said to Mum and Dad. Sue suggested that I might like to get John and Freddie organised in Leighton Buzzard, and then go to stay with Mum and Dad to try and sort them out. It seemed to be a sensible idea, as Sue had two young boys, and a business to run.

Freddie had been at the supermarket for two weeks, and he was getting on very well. John was working in Milton Keynes, so it was feasible. I made lists for everything; instructions on how to use the washing machine, the oven, and every appliance in the house! The freezer was filled to bursting, and little sticky-backed notes were everywhere. I loaded my little car on the Saturday evening with dog food, Wellington boots and luggage for all eventualities. Poppy and I set off for Lymington at 6 a.m. on the Sunday morning. I wasn't a confident long-distance driver. The boarding school situation had meant I had done several journeys round the M25, and I had been up and down the M1. I figured that early on a Sunday morning the roads would be quiet.

When I arrived at 'Franfay', our family house for many years, I was shocked to see how much Mum had deteriorated. Dad seemed unable to cope with the responsibility, and worried himself sick about what was happening. The family doctor, whilst having a serious chat with Dad in the kitchen, had said, 'We have a very sick little lady upstairs.' Dad had a bottle of methadone to give to Mum for pain, and a 5 ml plastic spoon. He also had some anti-fungal medicine to give Mum for her mouth, and a 1 ml spoon. The first thing I discovered was that he had the spoons the wrong way round, and Mum was getting five times too much anti-fungal, and one-fifth of the painkiller. He was mortified when I explained it to him, and relieved to hand everything over to me.

Mum had been in bed for some time, too weak to sit out in a chair, other than for making the bed. Her heels were sore, and bed sores were appearing. Her voice had become very deep and croaky, and it was getting difficult to understand what she was saying. Swallowing was difficult for her. She couldn't drink anything like water, it had to be thicker, and milk through a straw seemed to be the best option. The trouble was, being winter, the heating was on to keep her warm, but Dad had been leaving glasses of milk by the bed, and they had been turning sour. I introduced a flask of cold milk, and just a little in a glass at a time. Food was difficult, and Dad had been resorting to giving her baby food, which was very bland and tasteless. It was a case of trial and error to see what she could, or could not, eat. Custard seemed to be good, and I discovered she liked a little mashed avocado pear. I tried blending all kinds of things in a borrowed liquidiser, but her favourite was apricots. They were available in the supermarkets as Christmas was approaching, so I took to cooking and skinning them, and then liquidising.

Mum requested that Dad and I eat our meals on trays in her

bedroom, and it became our regular routine. We were sitting round on such an occasion when the GP called. He was a friendly Scottish man, in his late fifties, but he did have a tendency to prescribe whisky for all ailments. He spoke to Mum and told her he thought it would be a good idea if he requested the district nurses to call and treat her bed sores. He would also ask them to fit Mum up with a syringe driver on her wrist, which was like a little bracelet. The driver would have a button on it that Mum could press whenever she wanted another shot of painkiller.

I took the doctor downstairs to show him out, and give me the opportunity to talk to him. He very gently told me what I had figured out, and that was that Mum was seriously ill. Nine years earlier she had received surgery to remove a breast cancer lump, and the cancer was back. He said it was in her throat this time, and was spreading everywhere. The fluid building up in her chest cavity had probably caused the little heart attacks. He asked if I was able to stay for a few weeks, because he felt I was needed, and Mum would certainly not see the spring. He promised me backup, he would get the nurses coming, and he would keep an eye on the situation.

I obviously passed all this information to my sister, but we kept the detail from Dad. Mum hated hospitals, and Sue and I agreed between us that I would stay, and she would visit each morning when she had dropped her boys at school. That was just what I needed to give me a break. It was my hour for walking round the sea wall with the dog, and recharging my batteries. I had come prepared with large quantities of my 'go pills' and essential supplements, and Sue was keen for me to speak up if I needed more help.

Mum was still unaware of the fact that the cancer was back. We would have chats as I sat at the bedside, 'chats' meaning I did most of the talking, and Mum croaked what she could. Dad, being slightly deaf, was unable to understand what Mum was trying to say, and most people seemed to have the same trouble. Perhaps because I had spent years helping Freddie with speech therapy, and had been around children without much speech, I was able to become Mum's interpreter. The days of East Croydon station had been of use after all!

It was on one of these quiet occasions on our own when Mum asked me, 'Do you think I will get better?'

I couldn't tell her 'No'. I couldn't tell her she would get better, that would have been just as heartless. I was in a corner, and I had to think fast. I just said, 'Well, I am not a medical person, Mum, I don't know. But you have an appointment card for the hospital for the 15th January, we can ask the doctor then.'

She didn't say any more, but from that time on she knew she was dying. She knew me well, and the fact that I didn't promise her she would recover gave her the answer. I didn't realise straight away that this was the case, but from that time on, her questions changed.

As the doctor promised, the nurses came, and Mum seemed to understand the purpose of her syringe driver. They helped with creams and lotions for her sore heels, and brought extra soft pads for the bed. Mum was in the double bed, and Dad still slept beside her at night. Sleep was becoming a problem for him, he wasn't sleeping well beside Mum. He was getting her milk for her in the night, and generally being disturbed. He was getting very tired. One of the nurses suggested we could get a Marie Curie night nurse in to sit with Mum, and Dad could get some sleep in the spare room. I thought this was a good idea, and Dad finally agreed. The nurse came, sat in the armchair in Mum's room, and left at 6 a.m. in the morning. Mum was not a happy bunny. She objected to having a stranger in her room at night, especially when she rattled her sandwich wrappers. Dad didn't seem to sleep well in the spare room either, so that was the end of that little experiment, and the nurse never came again. I persuaded Dad to let me take a turn with him when it was all getting too much, and then I must admit I didn't get much sleep.

Mum managed to communicate to me one morning that in the night she had seen a lady standing at the bottom of the bed. Had I seen her? I had to admit I hadn't. I asked Mum to describe her, and she managed to say she had blonde hair in a short straight style, and had a kindly smile on her face. She had seen her several times, but she didn't mind her being there as she looked so friendly.

When Sue arrived I told her, and we looked at one another puzzled. 'Could be the drugs?' we said, and knew that was what Dad would say. We both had the same thought. Was it our other sister, Jackie? Jackie was Mum and Dad's second daughter. I was the eldest, and Jackie was born when I was two. She was a beautiful baby with blonde hair and blue eyes, but she died in Great Ormond Street Hospital, at age 18 months, from leukaemia. It was a terrible shock for Mum and Dad, and I always suspected they hadn't grieved properly, as her name was never mentioned.

Mum slept a lot whilst I was with her. I had been reading a book about a medium during those hours. In the book it mentioned that young babies and children, who die young, continue to grow up in the next world. I told Sue what the book said, and that was what made us wonder if the blonde lady was Jackie.

Mum started to ask me questions such as, 'Where am I going? I believe there is a heaven, but how do I get there?' I realised that when you come to terms with the fact you are dying, that must be the thing that interests you, and worries you, the most. Mum had been brought up by parents who were Salvation Army officers. Her childhood had been one of constantly moving from place to place, and school to school, as her parents were moved around the country every year. She had lived in very deprived areas in the Welsh Valleys, and the East End of London. In the Second World War she had helped her father run soup kitchens, as her mother had died young.

She married Dad, and after the war he worked for the National Provincial Bank. He was moved around in the London area. When Jackie died it was a big blow to them, and then I developed osteomyelitis in my leg at age five. I was in hospital for a couple of months, and Mum and Dad were told I would never walk again. It affected them terribly, coming hard on the heels of losing Jackie. As it turned out, I walked out of the hospital, thanks to the skill of the surgeon who nicknamed me his 'miracle girl' and admitted his surprise at my recovery. After leaving hospital I was sent to a school for 'poorly children' in Kingston-upon-Thames. It was called Kingston Open Air School, and it seemed to consist of us all being made to lie down on beds in the playground. I can remember the big heavy brown blankets they put over us, and the spoons of malt we had to swallow. I hated it there, and Mum wasn't happy about it at all. Mum felt bad things had happened to them since they had been living in Surrey, and she wanted to move away. Dad applied to the head office of the bank for a move to a place where I could have sea air. Somewhere in the south of England, anywhere, as long as it was near the coast. The bank obviously listened to the facts about Jackie's death, and my illness, and within a short time Dad was asked if he would like to open a new branch of the bank in Lymington, Hampshire.

When we first moved into 'Franfay' my Salvation Army

grandfather lived with us for a while. He was of retirement age by this time, and he must have been a big help to Mum. Sue was born three weeks before we moved to Lymington. This meant Mum was in a different house, in a new area, coping with a new baby and a seven-year-old, and probably a lot of packing cases. Grandad was a quiet, gentle soul, loved and respected by everyone who met him. Sue and I adored him. He would go off quite often to work in places like Dorking and Bognor Regis, anywhere he could still be useful to the Salvation Army. He was retired, but in name only; he never did stop working. After a while he bought a little old bungalow made of railway carriages, near Bognor Regis, and as children we loved staying there. Mum had this firm religious upbringing, and she believed totally in a heaven, but it just goes to show that however strong your belief, and your conviction, when you are looking death in the face you must have a few questions. In Mum's case they were practical ones, like, 'How do I get there?'

I talked to Mum about the book I was reading, and her first reaction was, 'Your grandfather would not have approved.' I hated to think I was doing something my wonderful Grandad would have disliked, but this book was beginning to answer questions for me. Despite the fact that Mum had been brought up in the Salvation Army, myself and my sister had been sent to the local church school, and we were versed in the ways of the Church of England. I had an enquiring mind, being fairly nosey by nature, and I can remember giving our local vicar a hard time at the confirmation classes. I wanted to know what people did in heaven all day, and how crowded it was in heaven! What was supposed to happen on the Day of Judgment, were the tombstones going to open up, and people all pop out like magic? He must have thought I was the candidate from hell! All he could ever say to me was, 'All things will be revealed', and

'You must have faith'. I was sure he was right, but I always wanted more detail.

In the book about the medium's life it was talking about what I referred to as 'heaven' as the 'Spirit World'. It was saying we live more than one life on Earth. We have soul groups, and we plan to come down to the Earth together in our groups to help one another. We make a chart before we come, setting out the challenges we want to overcome and learn from, so that we hopefully make spiritual development from each life. Each time we die we return to this 'Spirit World' and we review the life we have just lived. We judge ourselves on our behaviour, and if we are dissatisfied we have to come again, and try to do better next time.

Mum was interested in all this, and each day wanted to know more about my reading. I realised the book was produced on a cassette tape, and I knew Freddie had a personal cassette player in his drawer at home. John and Freddie were coming at the weekends and bringing large bags of washing for ironing. They brought the cassette player, and I managed to get the tape sent through the post. I set Mum up with the headphones, and loaded the cassette, and she just listened to the book.

I think that book must have been one of Mum's last pleasures. She didn't listen for long at a time, but it interested her, and she looked forward to each new chapter. She would pat the bed at the side of her gently, and ask me to sit and talk to her about it. At the very end of her life, here she was listening to something that was a revelation to her. We talked − or I talked, and she croaked − about what it must be like in the Spirit World. The book was telling us how all the colours are much brighter than on Earth. When you arrive you are taken by the hand of a loved one, and you go into a meadow of wild flowers, the colours of which we cannot imagine on Earth. In the meadow we are reunited with our friends and family who have all died before us. Not only do we meet up with our human family, but we can expect a wonderful welcome from our pets as well.

Mum was doing a lot of thinking, but she was slowly sleeping more and more. Her voice was getting weaker, and we could see her deteriorating. The doctor and the nurses were regular visitors, and we were getting to know them quite well. One day, Sue was with Mum and Dad in the bedroom when I returned from my regular walk with Poppy. I joined them and we were chatting as usual. Mum signalled to me that she wanted me to interpret for her. She wanted to talk to all of us about her cassette book. It was during this discussion that I suggested we set up an experiment. Mum knew she was dying, and we all knew, so we could talk openly.

I said, 'Why don't we agree on a secret code word that Mum can communicate to us to prove she has arrived in the Spirit World safe and sound. I will volunteer to research a good, genuine medium. I will give Mum a year, and then have a private reading with the medium to see if we get the code word.'

Mum said she was happy to do that. Dad thought we were lunatics, and my sister thought it a good idea. We brainstormed a few ideas for the code word, and came to the conclusion it had to be something a medium wouldn't say in conversation. It also had to be something pertinent to our family. I think it was Dad who suggested 'tambourine' because of the connection with the Salvation Army. Mum was not happy with that. She was a shy, quiet lady, and she didn't want to commit herself to dancing around with a tambourine. From that we went to the two words 'Salvation Army'. Surely a medium wouldn't say that by mistake. It was decided: those two words would be our secret code, and we were not to tell another living soul. It was just between the four of us, and then it would be our proof.

5

Saying Goodbye

Christmas was approaching at speed. It was something that was going to pass us by, as Mum was now so weak. Swallowing was a big problem for her, and she was failing fast. The GP came to visit, and as he was going to Scotland, assured us his partner would be holding the fort and had all Mum's details. John and Freddie arrived on Christmas Eve, and we were doing our best to be cheerful. Sue was going to cook a Christmas dinner at her house, and insisted John and Freddie should join them. I tried to persuade Dad to go as well, but he wouldn't hear of it. Instead I agreed a compromise, as usual, and I cooked a small piece of turkey, with some stuffing and vegetables, for Dad. I went to Sue's on the understanding that I would come back in the afternoon, and he would go and spend some time with his grandsons on Christmas Day.

Boxing Day turned out rather differently. After the usual visit from the district nurse, Mum made me understand that I was to gather the family round in her bedroom. I was acting as her interpreter, and she asked us why she was still alive. We all looked at one another, puzzled, and then I realised what she was asking. The GP had promised her that he would see she didn't suffer. He persuaded her to have the syringe driver on the basis she could give herself shots of painkiller whenever she needed them. What he hadn't said was that there was a limit to how much morphine the syringe driver would dispense in a given time. She had believed he was, as she said, 'putting something in the syringe driver'. I had to explain the situation to her, and she was quite upset. She asked us all to leave the room and come back in one by one. It was like something from an old black and white film. She said goodbye and took our hands and said, 'Thank you.' It was really quite upsetting for all of us. To me she said the same thing, but added, 'I won't forget', meaning she knew the secret code.

The next morning, the 27th December, when the district nurse came, being Christmas, it was someone we hadn't seen before. Mum just begged her to help her die. The nurse, who was obviously used to all situations, just breezily said, 'They are full upstairs at the moment, but when they want you, they will send for you.' After that Mum seemed to slip into a deep sleep. It was a bright sunny morning, the birds were singing, and it looked as if spring had come early. Dad insisted he would sit with Mum, and I was to go for a walk with John, Freddie and the dog.

We wandered round Lymington, and it was very pleasant. There were lots of people around, and there was a holiday feel to the place. When I returned, Dad was sitting beside Mum, who was in a very deep sleep by now, but making a noise in her throat. I sent Dad away to get some fresh air, and I sat with Mum. By mid-afternoon the noise she was making had become very loud. It was a horrible noise, and at the time, never having heard it before, I didn't recognise it as the death rattle.

I told Dad I thought we should call the doctor, and about an hour later the GP came. It was a partner in the practice we knew as Dr Ivor. He looked at Mum and said, 'I want to give her an injection.' Being on his own, and Mum being so poorly, he asked if I could help him by holding Mum's arm. When he had given the injection we left the room. He said he thought Mum only had a few hours. If anything happened I was to call him, but if we reached nine o'clock that evening and Mum was still with us, I was to phone him anyway.

I saw him out. He was very gentle, and sympathetic, and I thanked him and went inside to speak to the family. I phoned Sue to come, and she sat beside the bed with Dad and myself. The injection had calmed the noise, and Mum was now looking much more peaceful. We held her hand and watched as the vein on her neck gently pulsated. It was getting close to 7.30 p.m. when I decided I really should make everyone a cup of tea, and see that John and Freddie were getting themselves some food. It must have been only five minutes later that Dad came downstairs to tell me Mum had gone.

We all knew it was coming, we were all thankful she was out of her suffering, but somehow the reality of the fact she had left us still came as a shock. I couldn't believe that the very moment I stepped out of the room was the moment she actually died. I hugged Dad, and we went upstairs to Sue. We sat round looking at Mum, and I was amazed how quickly the colour had drained from her face, and how her skin had taken on a wax-like quality. Sue explained to me that the little vein we had all been watching had just stopped. Mum's hand was still clutching a tissue. It was so hard to take in. I would be lying if I said we didn't feel relieved; we all felt a sense of relief. It is just that you feel guilty for feeling that way. I removed the battery from Mum's syringe driver. What made me do that I don't know, I suppose I felt I ought to be doing something.

I went downstairs and phoned Dr Ivor. His wife answered the phone and was very professional, giving me her condolences. She said as soon as he returned from a call he would come round. He soon arrived, and asked us all to wait in the lounge while he went upstairs to Mum. He closed her eyes, and put her into a straight position, lifting the sheet over her face.

When he returned he sat on the sofa in the lounge, and took out the papers from his briefcase. He looked at all of us and said, 'You should be so proud of yourselves. You have been a wonderful team. Your Mum wanted to stay at home. and die in her own bed, and you gave her that wish. You made it possible. Not many people are that lucky. I just hope when my time comes I will have a team like you around me.' Then with a smile he said, 'I somehow doubt it.' He made us all feel better, and handed me the death certificate, and instructions for the undertakers, and left.

We all looked at one another in disbelief. My way of handling it was to spring into action, and think what had to be done. Looking back, I think I used undue haste, but grief affects people in different ways. I phoned the undertakers, who said they would be straight round, so I phoned the neighbours, just in case they saw the undertakers' van.

Once they had gone I realised Dad was going to want to sleep in the double bed that night. That sounded awful to me. Mum had died in the bed only hours before, and he was going to try to sleep in it. I pointed this out quietly to Sue, and we asked Dad what he wanted to do. His attitude, in his dazed state, was that it was his bed, and the sooner he got used to sleeping in it on his own, the better. Sue and I stripped the bed, remade it with clean sheets and different covers, threw open the windows, and took away all the paraphernalia that had been there to help Mum. I don't think any of us had much sleep that night, and we knew there would be a lot to do the next day.

We were all pretty glum at breakfast. I felt sorry for Freddie, so many changes in his life in such a short time. He had only recently adjusted to living back at home, then entered the world of work. I had gone away, and now his Gran had died. For Asperger's people, routine is of paramount importance, so this was a lot to cope with. They don't find it easy to show emotion. Now that we knew Freddie had Asperger's Syndrome, things were beginning to make sense to us, as we gradually learnt more and more. He just looked at us when he heard Mum had died, and had no idea how to react. Looking back, it had been the same when we were all so upset about having Rupert put to sleep. Freddie had made a daft remark about there being more room in the house without Rupert, a remark that irritated us slightly as we didn't understand. Another side to Asperger's is the lack of social skills. They have no natural instinct how to behave socially, and coupled with the lack of emotion, the loss of a loved one is something very perplexing. I just wanted to be able to spend more time explaining things to him, and making sure he was all right, but I had Dad to support, and Sue and I had a funeral to organise.

John and Freddie had to head back to Leighton Buzzard as they were both due back at work the next day. I sent them back with their shirts freshly ironed, and on hangers, and plenty of sandwiches to eat. It wasn't a case of sending them back with Christmas leftovers, because Christmas had passed by 'Franfay'. Our Christmas cake was sitting in a tin in the cupboard in Leighton Buzzard, minus any marzipan or icing. I made a list of black clothing for them to bring me from my wardrobe, and reassured them I would phone. It wouldn't be long before they were back for the funeral.

Dad was adamant that his priority that day was to draft an obituary for the local paper. I wasn't sure he was up to it, but it would give him something to put his mind on, and we duly unearthed his ancient 'sit up and beg' typewriter from a cupboard. One of the district nurses drew up outside the house, and came heading for the front door with a cheerful smile. I realised news hadn't filtered down to her, so I went out and broke the news where Dad couldn't hear. Obviously she was sad, but also embarrassed, and hugged me, and said very comforting and sympathetic things. I had held myself together until then, I had been the leader of the pack, the sensible, practical one, making sandwiches, and busy, busy, busy. Sympathy was the trigger that opened my floodgates. Over the weeks we had grown close to the nurses, we had got to know them, and we had our favourites. They were all much more caring than we had noticed, watching over the family as well as their patient. Now that Mum had gone, so had our daily support from these wonderful ladies.

Sue arrived, and we all had a hot drink, and a weep. The undertaker had made an appointment to come and see us that afternoon, which we appreciated as it was a Sunday. We knew we had to get our thinking straight, and decide a few things between ourselves before he arrived. We were all agreed that our first priority was to phone our cousin Marilyn in Devon, as her husband was a Methodist minister. If David could handle the emotion of conducting the funeral service, it would be great to keep it as a family occasion. We contacted Marilyn and David straight away, and they were really supportive, and David said he would make arrangements about the church. We knew Mum wanted burial, as a few years earlier she had insisted on buying two plots in the local cemetery. She wanted to think we could all eventually be buried together.

Sue said she wanted to leave the rest of the organisation to Dad and me, and she would go away and bake. That was her way of grieving, getting out the baking tins, and busying herself making the refreshments for the funeral reception. I was happy she was willing to take that on, as the last thing I fancied doing was spending hours in Mum's kitchen baking cakes.

The undertaker came, and Dad, visibly shaken and looking very frail, sat round with us in the lounge to make decisions he had hoped would never fall to him. What kind of coffin? Did we want Mum dressed in a robe? If so, what colour, which church were we using, which day, what time, which hymns, how many cars? It was all a whirl to me, let alone Dad.

The next task we faced was phoning everyone who needed to be contacted. I made a list, and with the aid of Mum's telephone number book, and her Christmas card list, I started to do the phoning. Mum's death was not that long after Princess Diana's funeral, and we had read how her Christmas card list was used to make sure all the right people were contacted. It is amazing how a fact that seems trivial when you read it can stick in your memory and become so useful.

The date for the funeral was set for Monday, 5th January 1998. The weather had been unseasonally mild and bright over Christmas, but as we entered January it became cold, wet and very windy. I took Dad to the Registry Office, which in those days was in Lymington, and we sat in a dull little waiting room, with other folk who were obviously as distressed as us. It was all very formal, very English, as nobody spoke to anybody else. We all silently took our turn. When it came we went in to see the Registrar and we answered the questions. The Registrar carefully wrote the Death Certificate. It felt very final, and 'conveyor belt'.

The wind turned into a howling gale, and rather than brave the supermarket for provisions, I decided to take Dad home via 'the little shop', as we called it. It was the local corner shop, a short distance from 'Franfay'. I pulled the car up outside, and Dad opened the door to get out. The wind caught the door and blew it wide open. As it did so the pin in the hinge of the door was forced out, falling on the ground. Fortunately Dad saw where it went, picked it up, and after a struggle, managed to get it back in place so that the door would shut. Dad remarked that it wasn't in properly, and he would look at it when we arrived home. In our hurry to get inside the house, and out of the wind and rain, we did nothing about it, and I made a mental note to get John to look at it.

John and Freddie returned with all the black clothes I had carefully listed.They had also brought their funeral attire, and it was good to see them back in Lymington. Freddie seemed to be coping, and John had spoken to Freddie's section manager, who sanctioned bereavement leave for him for the funeral. Dad had insisted he needed a new coat to wear, so I took him on a tour of the men's clothing shops in Lymington High Street. Not a lengthy process in Lymington, and miraculously we found him something dark and warm.

The morning of the funeral, Dad, John, Freddie and myself set about moving chairs around, and laying tables to prepare 'Franfay' for the reception. We put out as much of Sue's home baking as we could, and set out cups and saucers on the kitchen table. We were as organised as possible, for the family to return after the service. It was good that we all had something to keep us busy before the cars arrived at 11.45 a.m. Annabelle had arrived with her partner, and Sue and her family had gathered with us. Two of Mum's elderly cousins also arrived at the house.

We were all standing waiting when the hearse and cars drew up. It was so windy that the trees were almost bent double. I don't know what force number the gale was, but it was wild. The rain was coming down in buckets, and being whipped into our faces by the wind. The radio had been giving out news of railway lines being affected, and roads being closed because of falling trees. It was the sort of day when you don't even attempt to take an umbrella, unless you want to be Mary Poppins. We all ran down the path to the waiting cars, clutching our clothes around us.

We had worked out in advance who was going in which car. Before we shut the front door it was a question of making sure the rooms with food had closed doors, so that Poppy didn't eat all the goodies before our return! It wasn't far to the little church, and our cousin Marilyn and her minister husband were waiting at the door to greet us with hugs. Also waiting to greet us with her support was Angela, an old friend of mine. She was doing the verger's job that day, and it was great to see her.

Angela and I had shared a very small bedsit above a grocer's shop in London. They were our first early days in London, before I moved into Belsize Park, and Angela to West London. We didn't have many facilities, as they are called these days. We had to share a bathroom with the two guys who lived in the room above, the landlord, and another lady called Joan. We didn't have a kitchen, we each had a mini cooker called a Baby Belling. We have laughed many times about the amazing meals we managed to cook with just that tiny piece of equipment. We used to lie in bed and watch our Sunday dinner cooking! The decoration in the room would have been more appropriate in a fairground. The bedsit was situated on a corner of the Finchley Road, but at the time the traffic noise didn't seem to bother us. One night we were woken by the burglar alarm bell, which was located outside our window. It belonged to the leather coat shop next door. Angela watched as the robbers walked calmly in and out of the shop, loading all the coats into the back of a van. I was in my bed with a sheet over my head, yelling at Angela not to show her face in case they started shooting at us!

The furniture had seen better days, and after many months of

71

sleeping on a very elderly bed, my back started to trouble me. One night in desperation I moved the mattress and bedding onto the floor. In the morning it was our usual rush to get to work. When we came home that evening we found the landlord had used his key to get into our room. He had left us a note saying:

Wendy and Angela
I am disgusted with this room, never have I seen such a pigsty.
Get the mattress off the floor and on to the base, and get this room thoroughly cleaned, or find other accommodation.
This is the worst kept room I have ever seen.
Signed

We were annoyed that he had been in without prior warning, and found his note using the word 'pigsty' hilarious. I can't remember which one of us suggested doing a moonlight flit, but the thought just tickled us, and we laughed and laughed. Then we said, 'Let's do it, cheeky beggar, can you imagine his face when he comes in tonight if he finds us gone!' More and more hysterical laughter.

We knew our landlord was out, as when he closed the shop he always went round to see his lady friend for a meal. He was probably in his fifties, and seemed to be a very old man to us. He was extremely serious, and his conversation always revolved around the church, and how he gave people healing. Being a grocer, he had a tubby build. He always stressed how lucky we were to be living in one of his bedsits, as he only took people connected to the church. That amused us, as our link was rather tenuous. Angela had a friend, whose sister had a husband studying at the local Theological College, and a word from him had been our passport.

The more we thought about packing and leaving before late evening, the more it appealed to us, so we made a plan. In the yard behind the shop there were literally dozens and dozens of empty cardboard boxes of all shapes and sizes. The landlord would unpack his oranges, write a label that said 'Sweet and Juicy', and then just throw the empty box out of the door. We crept down the old iron fire escape staircase, into the yard. We helped ourselves to the boxes, trying hard to suppress the giggles. We both phoned our boyfriends, who had cars, and asked them to come round and ferry us, with all our luggage. John was my boyfriend at the time, and he was living in a flat in an old Victorian building. The rooms were enormous, with very high ceilings, and for the three of them sharing it was rather rambling. Even better, it was only just down the other end of the Finchley Road. We promised we would only stay in their living room for a few nights while we sorted out new accommodation.

The boys were puzzled about our sudden hairbrained scheme, and even more amazed that we could not contain our laughter, finding it such a hilarious joke. We made them creep down the staircase with the boxes so they didn't alert the other tenants. Looking back, their patience with us must have been stretched to the limit, as they drove up and down the Finchley Road. When all our belongings were cleared from the room we wrote the landlord a note, something along the lines of: 'We have paid you two weeks' rent in advance, so take this as our notice. We don't owe you any money. We weren't impressed with you entering our room without permission, so we have gone.' We left the note stuck to the pay telephone which was on the wall just outside our door. Still laughing, we put our keys with the note, and the boys took us to John's flat.

The thought of the landlord's expression when he read the note kept us laughing for days, until Angela discovered she was rather short of underwear. In our haste we had left a whole pile of her knickers in the airing cupboard situated on the floor above our bedsit. We contacted Joan, and arranged a secret meeting after dark for the repossession of the knickers.

Cousin Marilyn's husband, David, conducted a very personal family thanksgiving service for Mum. The rain stopped while we were in the church, and a few rays of sunlight came through the stained glass window, and fell on the coffin. For someone of Mum's age, the church was quite full, and it was a great tribute that so many people had bothered to battle the elements that day.

After the service the family followed the hearse to the cemetery, at the other side of Lymington. We had all been dreading seeing the coffin lowered into the grave, and poor Dad standing beside me was making a very strong effort to hold himself together. I can remember whispering to him, 'That is not Mum in that box, it is her old body.'

Back at 'Franfay' there was a fair amount of chaos. Never having organised a funeral before, I hadn't arranged for any help in the kitchen, or someone to even put the kettle on. Sue ran round uncovering food, and thank heavens for Gwen, Dad's cousin, and Mum and Dad's good friend Mavis, who came to my rescue making tea and coffee. I think it was my first lesson in finding out who my real friends were. Janice had taken time off work and travelled from Salisbury, and had brought her husband's mother, who knew Mum and Dad well. Angela, now living back in Lymington, was also another rock for me. The house that only a couple of weeks before had been quiet, but for the doctors and nurses, was now brimming with people.

John and Freddie had to return to Leighton Buzzard that evening, so that they could go to work the next day. All the friends and family filtered away, some with quite long journeys to do in the less than ideal weather conditions. Sue returned home with a whole tin full of sausage rolls which I had forgotten to put out, and Dad and I were left alone with Poppy.

I had been away from Leighton Buzzard for a good many weeks. I needed to return home, but I was worried about leaving Dad. He was adamant that he had to start 'paddling his own canoe', as he put it, and he didn't want to go back to Leighton Buzzard with me. Sue had promised she would be keeping a sharp eye on him, and would be calling in the next day. The morning after the funeral, Dad was anxious for me to leave. It was as if he couldn't wait to start grieving on his own. I loaded my car, and Dad had his coat on before I finished putting Poppy in the back. He was on the front door step with his shopping bag in his hand. He intended to say goodbye to me and then go straight into town. Sue told me later that he had stayed out all morning, and eaten lunch at a café, before facing the house alone.

6

Hinge Pin

It was good to be home. It seemed I had been away for years rather than weeks. I now had to try to find my old routines again. At least I found some of my old favourite clothes in the wardrobe that I had forgotten I possessed. Poppy was pleased to see her garden and her house, although she had thoroughly enjoyed paddling in the shallow sea water, and dipping her head in to retrieve stones. Our daily walks along the sea wall, and the thinking time it gave me, had helped to keep me going. I had made several new acquaintances on those walks, people who shared the same routes at the same time. I fell into step with an elderly gentleman one day, and he began to talk about his life. I was enthralled with his stories, and something he said has stayed with me ever since. He said, 'Man must be as thick as treacle to have suffered as we did in the First World War, and then let it happen again with the Second World War.' It was back to walks across the fields, and beside the canal, when we were home.

There was plenty of washing waiting, to say nothing of cleaning and cooking. One of my first tasks was to go to the supermarket and refill the fridge. It was still cold, wet and windy, and Poppy hated being left in the house on her own, so I took her in the car to the supermarket. There was no hint or hope of sun, so she would be fine. We parked in the large car park, and I wandered off with my shopping list. When I returned with a large trolley full of food, I realised Poppy was in the back of the car, and I had part of the rear seat folded down. It wasn't a problem, it just meant I had to put the shopping on the front passenger seat. As I opened the door there was a strange sort of 'whoosh' sound, and I realised the hinge pin had come out of the door again.

I had forgotten to mention it to John, and nothing had been done since Dad had put it back in when we were outside the little shop. The car I had at that time was a little metallic blue Peugeot 106. The hinge pin was in the same blue colour. I searched around in the car, on the floor, down the seat, moved Poppy out, even looked in her coat. I couldn't find it anywhere, and I knew I needed it to get the door shut. It must be on the car park floor I thought, so I crawled around the filthy car park, but still no sign of it. Here I was with a mountain of shopping, and a dog, and how was I going to get home?

I pulled my mobile phone from my bag and thought about phoning the AA, telling them I couldn't get the passenger door shut. That was going to sound really stupid, and I could imagine the cries of 'Women drivers!' in the AA call centre. As it happened I didn't have any charge left on my phone. I had intended to charge it when I arrived home, but in the midst of homecoming, and unpacking, it had slipped my mind. What to be done now? I decided that if I could shut the door with one hand, maybe I could improvise by pretending a finger on my other hand was the hinge pin. I would take it away as soon as the door was about to shut. It was a dicey manoeuvre, and could have resulted in serious injury to my finger, but it worked. The door was shut, I loaded the shopping, and we drove home.

I drove in under our car port, and let Poppy out of the car

through the hatchback. I unpacked the shopping, and Poppy, myself and everything came in through the back door into the kitchen. Poppy went down the garden and rolled around, and I had another search of the car for the pin, but to no avail. I decided I would have to remember not to use the passenger door, which was going to be a nuisance, so I picked up the phone, which is in our kitchen, and ordered a replacement pin from the garage.

The shopping was all put away, and I decided I had earned a cup of coffee, and maybe after all the stress of the car door, a biscuit to go with it. I picked up the coffee in one hand, the biscuit tin in the other, and called to Poppy to come in. We made our way down the hall towards the front of the house, and into the lounge. There is only one door into the lounge, and my chair is in the far corner. As Poppy and I were approaching the chair I said to her, 'What is that on my chair?'

As we drew closer I could see it was a metallic blue colour, and it was the hinge pin! It was standing upright in the middle of the seat, defying gravity, and looking very cheeky! I stopped, and looked, unable to believe my eyes. I moved closer, put my coffee and biscuit tin down, and picked the pin up. There was no doubt whatsoever that it was the missing hinge pin. I looked at Poppy and said, 'I don't believe this, how can it be?' Then I shrieked, and scared the poor dog half to death, saying, 'Thank you, thank you, Mum, this is your doing!'

When John came home from work I regaled him with the story. He can't bear to think of anything mystical, everything is black or white to him. 'It must have been in your clothing, or your hair, and fell on the chair,' he said.

'Don't be silly,' I said, 'I saw it before I was close enough for that, and in any case it wouldn't have stood up on end like that.'

I was convinced, but John didn't want to know. He was more concerned about getting the car door to open and shut without any more nonsense.

I phoned Sue and related my story. She said, 'Well, something very strange happened to me today. I was in the kitchen, doors closed, windows closed, and I had a whole stack of books on the kitchen table. I was nowhere near them and they suddenly jumped up in the air, and all fell to the ground. I just looked at them and could not believe my eyes.'

We laughed and said, 'Perhaps Mum doesn't want to wait for a year to give us the secret code.'

Living opposite me was a dear old lady in her early nineties. Her husband had died a few years earlier, and poor Violet was unable to bear the grief. When he first died she didn't want to stay indoors in her bungalow, and used to walk around the streets of Leighton Buzzard, crying. She didn't have any children, and the only family she had was a nephew, who was 15 years younger than her. He lived a short walk away, and visited her several times a week, helped with her shopping, took her to the doctors and did all her paperwork.

As neighbours, several of us could see the nephew, who was not in good health, struggling to cope. Violet was desperately lonely, but despite everyone's best efforts at persuading her to move to sheltered accommodation, she was determined to stay in her bungalow. Myself and three other neighbours took turns in popping in to chat to her of an afternoon. We knew who had been in, and when, but her greeting was always the same. 'I am so pleased to see you, I haven't seen a soul all day!'

My next-door neighbour, Louise, knew Violet adored cats and birds. Violet would often talk about the cats in her life, but we knew she wouldn't be able to cope with a cat, and would worry what would happen to it when she died. Louise decided a budgerigar was just what she needed. She went to the pet shop, bought the bird, a cage, and all the equipment and seed needed. She stood on Violet's doorstep, with the cage behind her back, and knocked on the door. When Violet saw the bird I think she was a little shocked at first, but that bird went on to be the love of her life.

The cage was stood in the living room in pride of place, and the bird was named Joey. It was only a matter of days before she decided the cage was far too small, and despatched her nephew to the pet shop to get a bigger cage. He came back with a parrot cage; it was a huge thing, but Violet was much happier with that. She used to leave the cage door open, and we all became used to Joey whizzing round our heads when we sat in the living room. That lasted a short while, and then she decided Joey was lonely, and she needed to get him a mate. Once again the long-suffering nephew was despatched to the pet shop. He came back with Jenny. All was not sweetness and light with Joey and Jenny, so another cage was put alongside the first, and they had their own cages. The living room was beginning to look more like a pet shop, but if it stopped Violet from feeling so desolate, we all agreed it was worth it.

As we all popped in and out we would see one another at change of shift. The discussion turned to the fact we had been invited to a meeting at one of the houses in the road, to discuss setting up 'Home Watch'. We all agreed it was a very good idea, but Violet looked less than enthusiastic. 'I don't think I could go out on patrol in the dark,' she said. 'I couldn't take a turn at anything like that.' We assured her it wasn't about anyone patrolling the street, we would just keep an eye out for each other. We couldn't get out of the front door fast enough to have a giggle. The thought of Violet wearing a tin helmet, bayonet in one hand and bird cage in the other, as she patrolled up and down the road, tickled us for days.

Violet had been born and bred in Leighton Buzzard, and if you wanted any information about the town, she was a good person to ask. She had given me the book about a medium that I had been reading in Lymington. I knew I had to start my research for a good medium. I talked to her about the book, and asked her if there had ever been any Spiritualist meetings in Leighton Buzzard. She told me that a few years earlier there were meetings being held in a little old hall that belonged to the Quakers. It was called the Friends Meeting House, and I remembered having seen it behind the Alms Houses.

I had been home for a few weeks, and after doing my shopping I wandered round to the Friends Meeting House to see if there were any notices on display. I had the great good fortune to bump into the caretaker, and he told me there were still Spiritualist meetings held there, on the first and third Wednesday evenings in the month. I had never been anywhere near such a place before, and kept thinking about my beloved Salvation Army grandfather. I knew I had to begin somewhere, and this seemed like my best bet.

It was a cold February evening when I first entered the hall. I was on my own, as John was having nothing to do with it. I was quite shocked to see how old the hall was. It was very tiny, with a high ceiling, and reminded me of some old Mission Hall. There were about three rows of dark wood pews, facing what I would have described as a platform. I learnt it was referred to as the rostrum. On this there were two more dark-coloured, very old-looking pews, facing the congregation. There were a few chairs at the back of the hall, and a doorway into some smaller rooms. There was no altar, or font, nor any of the usual trappings of a church. On the wall behind the rostrum was a big old-fashioned clock. There were large, thin, high windows at the sides, but there was no stained glass.

There were probably about 20 people sitting in the pews, and as I walked through the door an elderly gentleman approached me. He greeted me with a friendly smile, and a handshake, and asked if it was my first visit. I suspect it was very obvious that it was my first visit by the look on my face. He handed me a hymn book and I took a seat.

The meeting started and the elderly gentleman who had greeted me walked from the back of the hall to the rostrum. Standing facing us, he said, 'For those of you here for the first time, I can assure you there will be nothing spooky. No lights will flash, and no chairs will shake. If they do I will be the first one out of the door.' Everyone laughed. 'That's what we like to hear,' he said, 'a bit of laughter. It raises the vibrations, and the Spirit World like to see us happy.' He then proceeded to introduce the visiting medium.

She looked around the congregation and asked selected people in turn if she could give them a message. She was guided to each recipient by seeing a light above the person's head. This light was not visible to anyone who wasn't clairvoyant. Each one said 'Yes', and she proceeded to describe the person she could see in spirit form, and tell them what she was being told.

The evening ended, and I was somewhat relieved that I hadn't received a message, as it was all so new to me. I left, and didn't know what to think about it. I don't know what I had expected, but it was very different from anything I had attended before.

A few days later I was chatting to my neighbour, Louise, and I told her where I had been. Her reaction was, 'Well, I wish I had been with you.'

I said, 'Are you serious?'

She said, 'Yes, of course I am, are you going again?'

'Well, if you want to go, yes, we will go together.'

In the following months we went to several of the meetings. Louise liked the friendly atmosphere. People always chatted to us, and we enjoyed it. There were only two a month, so we probably made about one a month. I was keen to talk to the regulars, and get their views on the different mediums. It was a different one each time we went, and it became obvious to us that some were better than others. The general opinion seemed to be that the most favourite medium around was called Ron Moulding, and he lived in Luton.

Violet was very interested to hear that Louise and I had been to the Spiritualist meetings, and always wanted to hear all the details. We could see that she was becoming more and more confused, and forgetful, but she was extremely good for her age. We had a particularly dark, wet day, and at two o'clock the next morning she phoned me. Fortunately we have a phone by the bed, and I answered quickly thinking there must be an emergency with Dad. In my sleepy state it took me a while to comprehend that it was Violet, just phoning for a little chit-chat.

The next morning I saw her closing her curtains at nine o'clock. I phoned her nephew and he came straight away. It turned out she had gone to bed early, woken an hour later, and thought it was day time. She had been up all night thinking it was a dark old day, and was just off to bed when I saw her closing the curtains. We all said what a good thing it was that she hadn't decided to catch the bus into town. She would have been waiting at the bus stop in the dead of night.

Freddie settled in well at the supermarket, and was enjoying his job. It was a shame he didn't have any local friends, but he never complained, and just tagged round with us. He happened to be at home the day Violet phoned me in a panic. 'Wendy, Wendy, Joey is not well, there is something wrong, please take him to the vet.' I dashed across the road to her, and said I would take him to the vet in town straight away. She insisted we had to take him in his huge parrot cage, and she would wrap a blanket round it. I flattened the back seat of my little 106, and Freddie agreed to ride holding the cage.

When the vet saw us, he asked what on earth we were doing with a budgie in a parrot cage, why hadn't we brought the bird in a box with little air holes. I felt pretty stupid, but explained it was the treasured pet of an elderly lady. 'He is called Joey,' I added.

The vet reached in the cage for Joey, who immediately pecked him hard. The vet swore at the bird, and we all laughed. 'Well I think you should rename this bird Josephine,' he said. 'She is egg-bound.' He said he would give her an injection, but he didn't hold out much hope she would survive.

Freddie helped me return with Josephine in the parrot cage, and we broke the news gently to Violet. We walked back over the road, and there was a phone call from Violet immediately. 'Wendy, Joey has fallen off his perch.' I raced back to Violet, and she was breaking her heart. She had the tiny bird in the palm of her hand, and was sobbing inconsolably. It was obvious that the vet's foreboding was right, and poor Joey was dead.

Violet's next-door neighbour came round and sat with Violet, and her nephew came. He said he would dig a hole in the back garden and bury him if that was what Violet wanted. All Violet wanted to do was hold on tight to the now cold and stiff Joey. I said I would go and find a nice box. I rummaged around and found an old shoe box that said 'Green Flash' on the side, and was left over from Freddie's school plimsolls. I put some bubble wrap in the bottom, and cut a square of dark red velvet from some old curtains I had in the loft. I took the Green Flash coffin across the road, thinking it was rather inappropriate for a blue budgie, especially as she had the misfortune to have been thought male all her life.

It was much later in the day before anyone could prise the bird from Violet's hand. Annabelle happened to be visiting that day, and all she could say was, 'What an awful fate for any poor bird, being buried in a box that had contained my brother's plimsolls.'

7

Proof

I phoned Dad every evening. He didn't have much to say, but it was just my way of keeping in touch with him. Sue visited him every day, and kept me advised of his progress. He had suffered from depression during his life, and had a history of heart attacks. Now in his eighties, we were worried how he would cope without Mum. He started by clearing out cupboards, and generally getting rid of the baking tins and kitchen equipment he felt he would never use. He installed a microwave oven in the kitchen, and set himself up with a daily delivery of a hot meal, from a little café in the High Street. If it needed a bit of reheating he would pop it in the microwave. On Sundays he went to Sue's house.

He had been a keen photographer, and loved developing, printing and enlarging his own photographs. 'Franfay' only had one bathroom, so Mum was never that pleased when it was taken out of use to become a darkroom. On his own, with only himself to please, he could put his photography equipment wherever he wanted. Ideal as this sounds, he had to cope with loneliness. He put a very brave face on it, but we felt he missed Mum dreadfully. He suffered from tinnitus, ringing in the ears, for many years, and in later life his eyesight was failing. He had been an active member of the community in Lymington, and he had many friends. His really good friend was Geoff, and Geoff called round to visit him often in those early days.

I persuaded Dad to come and stay with us in Leighton Buzzard as often as he wanted, and we included him in our holidays. Freddie had four weeks' holiday a year when he first started work. John planned his holiday from work around Freddie's, and being three and a dog, we would take Dad to make four and a dog. The first year after losing Mum, we took Dad with us to Cornwall. He loved being with us, and joined in everything, always suggesting places to visit and things to do. Gradually we included Dad in all our holidays, and he would tack extra weeks on the end to remain with us in Leighton Buzzard, before we took him back to Lymington.

Louise and I were making occasional visits to the Spiritualist meetings, and the end of the year was approaching. I can't remember how I came by medium Ron Moulding's phone number, but perhaps I looked it up in the phone book. I made an appointment for what is called a private reading. The lady answering the phone didn't want my name, number or to know anything about me. I was the ten o'clock lady, that was all she knew, and she certainly didn't know I would be travelling from Leighton Buzzard. I told my partner in crime, Louise, that I had made the appointment, and asked if she would come with me. She had no idea what the secret words were, but she knew we had a secret sign. She said there was no way she was going to let me go alone, so I was grateful for her support, especially as I didn't know Luton well and hadn't a clue where to find the address.

It was November, only eleven months after Mum's death, but I figured it was close enough to the 12 months we had agreed, and I didn't want to wait until after Christmas. The morning of the appointment was foggy, which wasn't the best start. We set off in my little blue car, with a map and a lot of excitement. We were slightly late arriving, but we pulled up outside Ron's bungalow in a very ordinary residential street.

Ron answered the door, and said, 'Come in, your Mum is here, and has been waiting for you.' I exchanged glances with Louise, and Ron's wife came forward to take Louise to wait in the sitting room. Ron showed me into a room, which I assumed to be his study, and as he sat at the desk he pressed the button on the tape recorder to set it running.

I was quite taken aback at first at the speed with which he was pouring out information. It was as if Mum was on the other end of a telephone line. 'I feel your Mum is a very gentle soul,' he said, and then launched into strings of detail about Mum and her final weeks. He said, 'Before she died she was not sure what would happen. She believed in heaven, and she was not disappointed. It was easy to go through the golden light. She said, "My illness was the way it was designed for my body to break down."' Ron said, 'I feel it was a happy release when she finally passed. She didn't feel pain at the end, the noise from her chest, although awful for us to listen to, wasn't painful for her. Her soul was partly lifting from her body at that stage, and she could see Spirit people around her. She just drifted peacefully, and was unconscious at the end.' She says, "Dying is easy, you leave the pain behind."'

Describing her illness, she said, 'My voice changed, and people had to listen hard to hear what I was saying. I had to drink through a straw. I could only swallow baby-type food, and I pointed to things. Nurses came in, but they didn't understand me like the family. I had no energy before I went, and I couldn't converse. I had problems with my mouth, but it is perfect now.'

She was talking about a baby who had grown up in the Spirit

World. She had also met up with her brother. Ron said, 'I get the feeling he was a jovial character, and wouldn't have believed in all this.' She also said there was a small dog with her. She talked about how she loved the blackbirds, and one of her favourite places was Yarmouth, Isle of Wight. She also mentioned Wales. Ron said to me, 'You have been putting flowers in a vase by her photograph.' She wishes people would do that, rather than putting them on the grave. Referring to the grave, she said, 'It's cold there, and I am not there.'

She had met up with my father-in-law. She said, 'He was angry when he arrived. He is still smoking. He says they couldn't stop him there, and they can't stop him here.' (My father-in-law smoked his own roll-up cigarettes, no filters, and died of lung cancer.)

She said, 'Your father will never believe this message. He would like to know I am fine, but he won't approve. He is very stubborn, thinks he doesn't need help, but he does. There are people who think you will go home with an evil spell on you. I just wish they would do what you have done, and find out that we live on. We are much more aware of what goes on than you realise. We are better placed to help with things from here. I am still part of the family. When are people going to understand we live on, they miss out so much not believing in life after death. Enjoy Christmas, we will be celebrating with you. Oh, I mustn't forget to say Salvation Army connections.'

Ron said, 'Take her love, my light has now gone.'

When Ron switched the tape machine off, I looked at him and said, 'You don't know what you have just said to me.' He looked at me wide-eyed. 'The words "Salvation Army" were agreed with Mum before she died. They were the words of our secret sign to prove it was Mum. Only myself, my dad, and my sister knew the words we had chosen.'

Ron gave a little shiver and said, 'You have given me goose-bumps. You are very lucky to have been successful with that little arrangement. You must have done it for the right reasons. Many people do the same thing, but they are just treating it as a game, and they don't get the words back.'

We walked out of the room, me clutching my precious tape, and into the room where Louise and Ron's wife were sat chatting.

They looked up, Louise looked at me with anticipation, and I just screamed, 'I got the secret code!'

Louise shrieked, and said 'You didn't?' and gave me a hug. Ron and his wife were beaming from ear to ear.

'What were the words?' asked Louise.

I said, 'Salvation Army.'

She just stood there trying to take in the enormity of what had just happened. 'Well I don't think anyone would have mentioned those words in general conversation.'

We hugged again, and Ron and his wife were saying, 'We are so pleased for you.'

We thanked Ron, and somehow navigated our way out of Luton. We were both on a high, and couldn't wait to get home to play the tape.

The first person I phoned was my sister, Sue. She was thrilled, and couldn't really believe it. I phoned Dad, and he said, 'Oh yes', but he wasn't taking it in properly, and as Mum had said he didn't really believe it.

I could think of nothing else for days. I went over and over it in my head, everything that had been said gave me so much to think about. The baby who had grown up in the Spirit World must have been my little sister Jackie. So Mum had met up with her brother, my Uncle Will. I always thought he was great fun; 'jovial' was a good word to describe him. Mum did love

91

Yarmouth. Living in Lymington, with the ferry terminal to Yarmouth on the Isle of Wight, means it is a really nice excursion for the day. It is somewhat expensive, so we always regarded it as a treat. The little dog must have been our little dog Bimbo. I loved him so much. Mum had met Tom, my father-in-law. How come he was still smoking?! The thoughts ran on and on, and I just wanted to know more.

Having been told by Mum that the family in the spirit world would be with us at Christmas, I threw myself into preparing for a really good celebration. Dad was coming to stay, and Annabelle and her partner were joining us, so we would make up for the sorrow of the last Christmas.

I took myself to the last Spiritualist meeting before 25th December, and the tiny hall was packed. There was a lovely atmosphere, with the smell of mince pies wafting through from the back room. I squeezed myself into a vacant place on a pew beside the aisle. I wasn't expecting to receive a message as I had not long been to Luton for my private reading. The medium that night was wandering around the hall, and delivering messages to people in the hall, rather than standing on the rostrum. I rather liked that as it gave each message more of a personal feel. I can remember the light touch on my shoulder as he walked down the aisle and approached me from the back of the hall.

'I have your mother here,' he said, 'she says you have a son who needs a lot of extra special looking after. She wants you to know that the Spirit World are very pleased with the way you have been caring for him. You have been doing all the right things, but you mustn't worry about his future. You are a big worrier, but please don't, it is all planned out for him, and he will be all right. She also wants you to know that your son chose you, and your husband, to be his parents, to help him through life. Take her love, and they will be with you at Christmas.'

On Christmas Day we were all sitting round the dinner table to eat our Christmas dinner. I raised my glass, and proposed a toast to Mum and all our family in the Spirit World. As I finished what I was saying, and we had our glasses to our lips, the lights in the dining room flickered, and we all laughed.

I was still on a high, thinking about the secret sign. Christmas was over, and the cold winter months were ahead. It was my routine to walk my beautiful golden retriever every day. Dogs need their exercise, come rain or shine, and I just lost myself in thought on our walks through the fields and woodland. I always felt safe with Poppy, following the pinning of the man against a tree incident, and now I was feeling even less alone. From what Mum had said through Ron, I imagined different members of my family enjoying the walks with us. Maybe dear old Rupert was with us. A little dog had been spoken about in the message, and I took that to be Bimbo. I was quietly thrilled that a dog had been mentioned, as it was proof to me that our pets also live on. I had heard things said in the parish church, when I was younger, about only humans having a soul, and then another reference to dogs being 'the furniture of heaven', whatever that meant. Comparing such beautiful creatures to a wardrobe or a sofa quite upset me! I am a great lover of dogs, our family dogs have always been a great source of joy to me. They give you unconditional love, and rely upon you like a baby.

I also thought long and hard about Mum's comment that her illness was the way it was designed for her body to break down. Mum had enjoyed good health most of her life, until she had breast lumps removed, nine years before her death. She didn't have extensive surgery, and no chemotherapy, just radiotherapy and medication. She had lived a normal life for nine years following the first awful realisation that she had cancer. My very good friend since the age of seven years old, Janice, had undergone extensive surgery for breast cancer about three years before Mum died. She had also recovered well, and had picked up the threads of normal life again. I worried how Mum's death from cancer must have upset her, as she knew the whole story. I had emphasised to her that the cancer that killed Mum was throat cancer, but I knew Janice wasn't stupid, and must have dreaded her cancer returning.

I resolved to look for some more books written by mediums, and to get to grips with my old question, 'What do they do in heaven all day?' As well as a lot of deep thinking, I turned my attention to my hair, which was fast making me look like a piebald pony. All my friends were developing a few grey hairs, and most were looking quite attractive in what I believe is termed the 'salt and pepper' stage. My hair for some reason was turning grey in large patches, whilst the rest remained brown. I had a grey fringe, and grey clumps around the back.

My hairdresser at the time was what is termed 'mobile'. She comes to you. I knew she was coming to cut my hair, so I thought I would visit the chemist before she came, and find some hair colourant that would cover grey. I found some in a very promising shade of blonde; it said it covered all grey hair, and was entitled 'Utterly Natural'. 'Just what I need,' I thought, and I planned to show the hairdresser and ask for her advice, just to be on the safe side.

Maureen arrived soon after John and Freddie had left for work. She snipped away, and when she had finished she inspected the pack of colourant. 'Looks good,' she said, 'but be very careful to cover all the roots. Pay particular attention to the roots.'

She left, and I headed for the bathroom to work on my new

look. I read the instructions, which was good, as I am apt to be a little impatient. Maureen's words were ringing in my ears, so I paid very good attention to the roots. So good in fact, that when I looked at the clock I had used up all the 'cooking time'. I wasn't sure what to do, so I hurriedly slapped on the rest of the colour, then I had this awful thought that if I left it on the roots for too long, the hair could break. I could end up with no hair at all! The thought was too much, so I rinsed it all off. When I looked in the mirror: shock, horror! Instead of being an 'Utterly Natural' blonde, I looked like a tangerine.

If in a crisis there is always the same solution: phone Louise. 'Come and have a look at my hair, please,' I begged.

Louise gasped when she saw me, and put her hands to her face. 'Don't panic,' she said, 'go into the bathroom, shampoo it, and rinse it, and do that twice. When you have done that, dry it. I will be back.' Unbeknown to me she then phoned Maureen and said, 'Get round to Wendy's house as soon as you can.'

By the time I had followed Louise's instructions Maureen had arrived. She took one look at me and could not stop laughing. Despite the extra shampooing I was a vivid shade of orange, and where I had just blown it dry with the hair dryer, I looked like Ken Dodd on a bad day. I thought Maureen's laughter would never stop.

She brought large boxes of colours from her car, and bottles of peroxide. She explained to me, as she was applying the new creams, that in washing the colour off too soon I had turned it into this very brassy colour. She dashed off to do somebody else's trim, and left me to calm down and let the potions work. When she came back she was relieved to see the tangerine look had gone, and she applied yet more mixtures. Again she dashed off to keep up with her schedule, and then back she came. The hair was finally washed, and she told me that by the time I had dried it, all would be well.

I think it was mid-afternoon by the time I was able to snatch a sandwich, and prepare food for the evening meal. I pulled a hat over my damp hair, and took the dog for a quick walk round the block. Once home I was finally able to dry it properly and see the finished colour. Louise popped back to see how it was all going.

I said, 'It is five o'clock and I have been doing my hair since ten o'clock this morning.' We looked at each other and dissolved into uncontrollable laughter.

'That is absurd,' she said, 'let's have a look.'

Maureen had done a good job, and amazingly the hair was at last looking sort of blonde. Crisis − and laughter – over, I concentrated on the evening meal.

As we sat in the kitchen eating, I said to John and Freddie, 'Do you notice anything different in this kitchen today?'

They looked all around, looked at me, and puzzled, they both said, 'No.'

'Could it be the colour of my hair?' I asked.

They stared, said 'Oh', looked unimpressed, and carried on eating their dinner.

All of the neighbours in the road continued their regular visits to dear old Violet. She had been looking very frail, and it seemed to us she was getting weaker by the day. Her nephew sent for the doctor, and he in turn sent the nurse to take blood. Violet then had various visits to the hospital, and cancer was diagnosed. She made it clear to everyone she did not want to leave her bungalow, so a care package was finally put together, and the carers came in three times a day. Violet was happy with the arrangement as it meant she had more company. In the summer John used to cut the grass in her front garden when he was doing our mowing. He would just push the mower over the road and cut her little patch. Violet thought this was wonderful.

She was issued with a walking frame. All the little team of visiting neighbours used to let themselves in and out, so that she didn't have to keep answering the door. She also had an emergency call button which she wore round her neck; well, when she was reminded, she wore it round her neck. She decided that in the event of an emergency, John and I should be the first on the list to be phoned by the emergency call service.

There were many occasions when the phone would go, and we would be asked to go and see what had happened. Fortunately John was usually around when the calls came, and we would hurry over the road to find her sitting on the floor. She would just slide down from her chair and John would be able carefully to get her back. As time went on she began to fall, and then we had to call the paramedics, as she needed to be lifted properly. It was always rather hazardous as Jenny, the remaining budgerigar, would be flying around over our heads. It would have needed only one person to innocently leave the door open, and Jenny would have made a bid for freedom. We dreaded the thought of anything happening to Jenny, as Violet would have gone into a decline had that happened.

Violet had already made her wishes very clear to all of us. If anything happened to her, she wanted her nephew to take Jenny to the vet, and have her put to sleep. Jenny's body was then to be put in her coffin. We all felt pretty uncomfortable with this request, but Violet was adamant that nobody else would keep Jenny in a parrot cage, talk to her all day, and let her fly free around the house. We couldn't argue with this, but it did seem rather harsh to place a death sentence on the poor bird. Even worse, we didn't envy the nephew who was made to promise her wishes would be carried out.

All this time I kept taking my big vitamin and mineral 'go pills', and pacing myself was always at the back of my mind. I was still in touch with a few members of the old ME support group. We used to phone each other in times of crisis for advice, and moral support. Times of crisis were usually if we picked up a virus, or some kind of illness, because that then makes the ME worse. Emotional upset is another flashpoint, so we keep in touch, and have the occasional coffee morning together. To this day I make sure I don't put myself into a crowd situation if I can help it. I don't generally go to the theatre, or the cinema, concerts, or places with large groups of people. I just allow myself small meetings, and train journeys at off-peak times. Of course there will always be a situation that arises when you find yourself in a group of people and someone starts coughing or sneezing. In those circumstances I usually surprise myself with the speed of my running.

Dad seemed to be coping with life on his own in Lymington, with the support of Sue, and he was spending quite long spells with us in Leighton Buzzard. Accommodation was not a problem as we had extended the house to provide an extra bedroom and bathroom for Annabelle when she was younger. Now that she and her partner had their own house, the extension was standing empty. There was a small 'sun room', as we call it, tacked on the end of the bedroom, so Dad in effect had his own annexe. It was separated from the rest of the house by the dining room, so it was ideal for Dad. We installed an extra television in the sun room, and made it into his own little sitting room, which opened out on to the garden. It was always in the back of our minds that if Dad decided he wanted more care, or company, we had the solution ready and waiting.

Dad loved to go away on holiday with us. He missed his coach trips with Mum, and in earlier years the cruises they took.

We booked an apartment that overlooked Loch Ard in the Trossachs, Scotland. As usual all of us, plus dog, were driven up the motorway by John. It turned out to be a beautiful place, and the weather was warm and sunny. There was a picnic table and chairs right by the side of the loch, and I used to pop to the local bakers, and take a spread of good things to eat down at the loch side. Poppy thought it was heavenly as she could dip her head in the crystal clear water, and retrieve great big stones.

In the nearby town of Aberfoyle, Dad had seen an advertisement for a sheep show. He was very keen for us all to go, so we duly took our seats, and waited to see a bit of sheep-shearing, or whatever. When it started, two very burly men appeared in kilts, and Viking-type helmets, and started joking with the audience. It became almost slapstick. Then one of the men came to the lady sitting next to Dad, picked her up, threw her over his shoulder, and took her offstage, kicking and screaming. Dad thought it was the funniest thing he had seen in ages, and didn't stop laughing about it for days. All the rest of the show with the sheep, and the different breeds, went right over his head.

He was walking with a stick and his knees were really beginning to trouble him a lot. Being very stubborn he didn't want to give in and go to see the doctor. He knew he would be letting himself in for surgery, and at his age he didn't want it.

8

End of an Era

We had taken Dad back to Lymington a couple of weeks after the holiday in Scotland. It was our routine to take him back on a Saturday, stay the night at 'Franfay', and return home on the Sunday. I had visited Violet on the Friday before we left. On the Monday morning as I opened the curtains I saw Jill, Violet's carer, going in, and then I saw her come out and start making a phone call. Immediately I suspected something was wrong, and it transpired that Jill had found Violet slumped over her chair, obviously having died that morning.

We were all upset at losing her, and I couldn't believe I hadn't been around for her last two days. Her nephew set to work to organise the funeral, and on 21st August, just a week later, we all made our way to the cemetery. Violet was 94 when she died, so at that great age there were not many of her friends left to attend the funeral. It was to be a simple service of thanksgiving in the tiny chapel at the cemetery, and burial afterwards, in the same grave as her late husband. Two carloads of neighbours parked at the cemetery, alongside the lady curate who was to take the service. She was very pleased to see us, and walk with us to the chapel, so that she could find out a little more about Violet's everyday life. We sang Violet's favourite hymns, and then the lady curate rendered most of us to tears. She said

Violet's nephew had told her we were the neighbours that most people could only dream of having.

We all missed Violet, she had become such a part of our lives, and we knew her bungalow would have to be cleared and sold. There was of course the situation with Jenny the budgie to be resolved. Violet's nephew didn't know what to do. He had promised Violet he would have the bird put to sleep, but it seemed such a dreadful thing to have to do. In the end he decided to talk it over with the vet. The vet listened to the story, and then looked at Jenny. The advice was that Jenny was very old by budgie standards; she may not have been that young when Violet gave her a home. He didn't think the bird would last very long in a different environment, so he felt it was no bad thing to carry out Violet's wishes.

The next request was not so easy to carry out. Violet wanted Jenny to be put in her coffin, but the undertaker had been quite adamant: 'No can do.' Whether it was a Health and Safety ruling, or what, we never did find out, but other arrangements had to be made. I believe Jenny's body was eventually buried in a place Violet's nephew felt appropriate. I often wondered what sort of a coffin that budgie had; probably not a box with a velvet lining that said 'Green Flash size 7' on the side!

I had been suffering with tummy pains for a few weeks. Just like Dad I wasn't over-anxious to dash to the doctor. A friend suggested it could be gallstones, and that rang a bell in my head. In the ME support group we were always being bombarded with different therapies, and I remembered our chairman being given a recipe for removing gallstones. How he came by it I am not sure, but it had the words 'Dulwich Health Limited' printed at the end.

It was entitled 'Gall Bladder Flush':

Drink 2 litres of fresh pure apple juice a day for five days, eating normally as fat free as possible. On the sixth day have no evening meal. At 9 p.m. take 1 or 2 teaspoons of Epsom Salt dissolved in 30 to 60 ml warm water.

At 10 p.m. mix half a cup (4 oz. 120 ml) olive oil with 2 oz.(60 ml) fresh lemon juice. Shake vigorously, or put in a blender, and drink all the lemon drink down. (It doesn't taste as bad as it sounds, it is just a thick lemon drink.)

Immediately upon finishing the lemon drink go to bed and lie on your right side with your right knee drawn up towards your chin. Remain in this position for 30 minutes before going to sleep.

This encourages the olive oil to drain from your stomach, helping the contents of the bladder and/or liver to move into the small intestine.

Next morning the stones will pass, will be green in colour, and soft as putty, varying in size from grains of sand, to some as large as your thumbnail. You will not feel a thing, but will be amazed at the results. Thousands have done this instead of major surgery. Even laser and keyhole surgery is not always successful. If you are not satisfied with the results try the flush-out a few days afterwards, or even double the dose of olive oil and lemon juice. It may be advisable to have a flush-out at regular intervals i.e. one or two years apart.

Please photocopy this sheet and pass it on to others.

John made a few remarks, such as, 'Would you like to put a saucepan on your head while you lie with your knees up?' I ignored his jest and followed the instructions.

The first time I did the flush it was disappointing, nothing happened, so not wanting to admit defeat I repeated it a couple of days later. The second time I could not believe my eyes. I had passed dozens and dozens of little green stones the size of my small fingernail. As the instructions had said, they were as soft as putty, and you don't feel a thing.

I was so impressed that I filled a specimen tube with the little beauties, and took them to show my GP. I asked her to confirm that they were in fact gallstones. She said there was no doubt, they were gallstones all right, and it was the funniest thing she had ever seen. I was rather insulted at her laughter, these were my precious exhibits, and I said, 'Well, I don't think it's funny. I think it is jolly good.'

Poor old Dad had also plucked up courage to visit his GP, and his outcome was not as simple as mine. An appointment at Bournemouth hospital, followed by X-rays of his knees, showed both his knees were worn out, and he needed replacements. He was told the waiting list was lengthy, and he would hear with an appointment in the fullness of time.

Our friends Janice and Bryan phoned to say they had applied to swap their time-share accommodation. They had been successful, and had secured a week in Devon. They asked if John, Freddie and I would like to join them. It was a dog-friendly cottage in a small courtyard of little cottages, within walking distance of the beach. They could take their Corgi, Muffin, and we could take Poppy. It sounded wonderful, so we readily agreed. Just before we were due to travel it was announced that the drivers of petrol tankers were going on strike We had a full tank of petrol, enough to get us there, but not there and back. We were feeling very unsure about it, but the word was that it would all be over by the time we wanted to return. We had discussions with Janice and Bryan on the phone, but they had a shorter journey than us, starting from Salisbury. We all decided the day before that things were looking OK so we would go.

We were a few miles from our destination when we found a small garage with petrol for sale. John filled the car up and we felt happier knowing we had enough petrol for the return journey. Janice and Bryan arrived just after us, and their tank was also topped up. The cottage turned out to be beautiful. It had originally housed a cider press, and had a gorgeous round sitting room with a galleried bedroom above. It led out through double doors on to a patio which looked out across farmland towards the sea. The cottage was named 'The Round House', for obvious reasons, and we were thrilled with it. We were down a quiet country lane, and had the use of a games room with a table tennis table, and a small swimming pool. We had a few neighbours in the other adjoining cottages, and it seemed a perfect base for exploring the South Hams of Devon.

Little did we know as we looked around the cottage that the petrol crisis was to become far worse. Instead of being all over by the time of our return, petrol was going to be unavailable. We all decided we had enough petrol to get home, so we would leave the cars in the car park. No exploring the South Hams by car, instead we would explore on foot. The weather was kind to us, lovely sunny days, and we would set off from the cottage in our shorts and T-shirts, with rucksacks on our backs, and dogs on leads. It was nearly September, and there was an abundance of blackberries in the hedgerows as we walked towards the sea. Our first port of call when we arrived at the beach was 'Uncle Rocky's' tea hut, as we called it. We soon discovered from the smell that Uncle Rocky dispensed the most wonderful chips. Fortified with chips we would walk along the cliff path to Hope Cove. This little cove is one of my favourite places. There are thatched cottages right down by the sea, and fishing boats pulled up on the beach. It really is picture postcard perfect, and we adored it.

Having been brought up near the sea, I have always loved it. Living in Leighton Buzzard, I don't think you can get much further from the sea. I treasure my days I am able to spend taking in the wonderful salty smell of the air, and paddling my feet in the gently rippling water. There was a small shop in Hope Cove, and one hotel had a large sign hung across the front advertising 'Devon Cream Teas'. John has always had a passion for sweet food, scones with jam and cream in particular. We all read the sign, and looked at one another. 'Shall we?' we said. 'Yes, we are on holiday.' We sat outside the hotel, dogs under the table, and tucked into the lashings of cream and jam. The portions were a very generous size, and we were all enticed to eat more than we should, especially as we had started out with a good helping of Uncle Rocky's chips.

We sat on the beach and generally relaxed, really enjoying the banter and the laughs. We had all been friends for so long, and spent many holidays together. Sometimes we laughed until our sides ached. We set back through the fields and lanes to our 'Round House'. We arrived back in time for evening meal, and Janice, who was a very good cook, produced a wonderful, very large, dish of lasagne. It was just too good to refuse, but on top of chips and a huge cream tea it was too much for me. My punishment for being so greedy was to be as sick as a dog, and everyone laughed.

We realised as the days passed that the petrol crisis was getting worse, and now the shops were beginning to run out of supplies. The next day we decided to trek to a shop attached to a petrol station, where we thought we could get bread and some fresh vegetables. When we arrived we were quite shocked to see how low the stocks were. We did get some bread, but we ended up buying dried yeast and bread flour as well, so that we could make our own. Janice and I always took a stock of food with us. We would agree beforehand who would take what, and we usually added a little extra, which proved to be a wise move. We didn't go hungry, 'Uncle Rocky' kept his supply of chips coming, and we walked miles. We all agreed at the end of the week what a good holiday it had been, and how we had enjoyed the walking instead of using the cars. We said our fond farewells, and headed home, and guess what: the next day the petrol strike was called off!

We returned to the news that Dad had a date for his knee replacement operation. It was some way in the future, but nevertheless a date. He couldn't understand why he was to have his operation on a Sunday, but we explained to him that these were drastic times for hospitals. Their waiting lists were so long that they were working extra days. Sue and I discussed the practicalities of it all, and it was agreed that I would go down to Lymington to look after Dad when he came out of hospital. Sue agreed to do the hospital visits, so we made our arrangements: we did lots of shopping and cooking to load our freezers.

Sue took Dad in to the hospital on the allotted Sunday, and stayed with him until he was ready for theatre. He had been 'nil by mouth' all day, he was in his hospital gown, and feeling sleepy with his pre-med, so she left, wishing him good luck and saying, 'I will see you tomorrow.'

She left and drove home, then a couple of hours later she received a strange phone call from Dad saying, 'Please come and pick me up.' Worried sick, she jumped in her car and drove the hour's journey to Bournemouth.

While she was driving, her husband, back at home, received a call from the hospital saying, 'We are very sorry, we don't want to worry you, but we have lost your father-in-law.' For a split second Sue's husband thought they meant he had died, but then he realised they were saying they couldn't find him.

107

In those days we didn't have mobile phones, so Sue could not be contacted. When she arrived at the hospital Sue found Dad very muddled, and in a drowsy state, leaning against the wall of the main entrance. He was sort of dressed, in an untidy, inside-out way, and she was horrified.

He said, 'Oh Sue, I am so glad to see you, my operation was cancelled, and they told me to go home.'

'What do you mean, cancelled?' she said.

'Well, the operation in front of mine took longer than expected, so they ran out of theatre time. I said, "Well, do I have to wait until the morning then?" and they said, "It doesn't work like that, you have to get up, get dressed, and go home. You will go back on the waiting list. We will try to fit you in within a month."'

Sue wasn't best pleased about it all, but her first priority was to get Dad home safely. She told him he would be staying the night at her house, and drove him back to Lymington. When she arrived home she was told about the hospital call, and how they couldn't find Dad. She immediately phoned the hospital to tell them Dad was safe and sound, if a little confused at age 86, and in a state of shock.

What made it worse was, it transpired a few days later, that while he had been in there he had picked up a chest infection that was named the 100-day cough. Dad returned to his own house feeling let down, and disappointed. Through the next three months he was fed antibiotics like sweets, and was very poorly, unable to even get back on the waiting list for his operation. Eventually he was given a new date for his surgery, and more surprisingly, a new location. The hospital had made arrangements for him to have his operation at a private hospital. They had become so behind with their operating list that they had rented time and space to get themselves back on track. The NHS nurses were sent to care for their patients, and took over a section of the hospital to work through a long list of surgery.

We told Dad how lucky he was to be going to a private hospital where he would get his own room, and own bathroom. Sue jollied him along, and finally he received his new knee. I wrote my sticky notes and placed them on the kitchen cupboards, and doors, and once more left John and Freddie to fend for themselves. Poppy and I installed ourselves in Dad's house, and I helped Sue bring him home from hospital.

Dad was very disorientated after the anaesthetic. He told us he had been planning to break out of the hospital at two o'clock in the morning, to catch a bus home. He could see a bus stop from his window. Thank goodness he wasn't physically capable, as the bus would have taken him in the wrong direction, and he would have gone deeper into Dorset. Another day he thought he was in the desert in Africa. Bournemouth has a lovely sandy beach, but the desert it is not!

Physiotherapy consisted of a few sessions in the hospital, and Dad being given an exercise sheet to follow at home. He found the exercises extremely difficult. While he had been on the waiting list to have his left knee replaced, his right knee had deteriorated rapidly. Sue mentioned this to the hospital before the operation, and pointed out the right knee was now worse than the left. She was told he was listed for the operation on his left knee, and if it was changed to the right knee, he would have to go back on the waiting list! The consequence for Dad was that it was very hard to walk at first, with the right knee being so useless. He was very good about his exercises, and with a little encouragement from Sue and me, and a lot of praise, he did very well.

As he improved I would take him out in the car of an afternoon, and we both liked to park by the sea at Keyhaven, just a short drive from Lymington, and watch the coming and going of the boats. I would take a flask of tea and a tin of biscuits. If the weather was suitable, Dad would sit on the bench and I would walk Poppy along the footpath, where I could keep an eye on Dad. The month was now September, and on the 11th it was a beautiful sunny day. I decided to take a picnic lunch as it was so nice, and a cushion for Dad to put on the bench. We lingered by the sea that day, it was too good to go indoors, and Poppy was enjoying it as much as us.

When we opened the front door back at 'Franfay' Dad walked into the lounge with his stick, and settled himself in his favourite chair. I followed and switched on the television. I was intending to sit down, but I looked at the television again, and thought, 'This isn't the right programme.' Then I saw the planes crashing into the twin towers in New York. I sat in the nearest chair, and there Dad and I stayed for the next hour. I don't think we spoke one word, we just sat gazing in disbelief. Finally one of us said something like, 'This can't be true.' While we had been peacefully sitting at the water's edge all day, this carnage and horror had been playing out in New York. It is always said, 'You never forget what you were doing on 9/11.'

Dad soon declared himself fit to cope on his own, and sent Poppy and me on our way back to Leighton Buzzard.

9

Reassurance

The following spring, Freddie had his allocation of holiday so we decided to take Dad to Wales. We found a self-catering holiday bungalow in Laugharne, not far from Tenby on the south coast of Wales. A pretty little township, where Dylan Thomas had lived. The views across the estuary were stunning, and Poppy loved the countryside and the beach. She loved anywhere she could plunge her head under water and retrieve stones.

I had been complaining of terrible pains in my back before we left, and everyone had been saying, 'Oh backache isn't nice.' The day we were due to leave, the car was loaded, and I just sat down in the chair and said, 'I don't know if I can do this.' John gave me one of his looks of total exasperation, and suggested we just drive round the block to see if I would be all right. I knew I wasn't at my best, but I didn't want to ruin our week away. When we arrived and unpacked we all had a meal and I took myself off to bed.

The following morning John said to me, 'What is that big bite on the top of your leg?' On investigation in the mirror the whole problem became clear. I had shingles. We took things quietly that week, I was too late for the shingles tablets, so I just had painkillers, but it wasn't one of our jolliest holidays.

Dad seemed on the face of it to be coping, and when we eventually returned him to Lymington I thought perhaps he really enjoyed a bit of peace and quiet when he was on his own. Sue was still visiting him every day, and for once things seemed to be on an even keel.

I had a surprise telephone call from a friend who had been very good to me in the early days of ME. She was another mother who I had met at the local school, and she had taken Freddie out and about with her son. She was now the office manager of a small communications company in Leighton Buzzard. I say small, I mean small. They worked out of a tiny office without room to swing a cat. She was looking for someone to do a few hours telephone monitoring a week. She had a whole team of people doing just a small number of hours, so that she could utilise different voices. It could best be described as the telephone version of the mystery shopper. We made calls to companies and evaluated how long it took for them to answer, and so on. It was quite a laugh, and I enjoyed it. I met new people, and the office manager knew my situation with the ME. It was all going well for me. A little job, and Freddie, although still living at home, was happily settled working in the supermarket. I had been having no more disasters with my hair. Since the tangerine hair incident Maureen was visiting every six weeks to cut and colour my hair. Life seemed to be a lot more simple and straightforward.

Still fighting the remnants of the 100-day cough, Dad had received more shock, and more blows. His sister-in-law and his cousin both died within a short space of time. Then at a routine visit to the optician he was told his eyesight was no longer good enough for driving. Living on his own, driving was his lifeline. The optician had been telling him for some time that his cataracts needed doing, but Dad didn't believe it. He was convinced there was nothing wrong with his eyesight. He said he had no intention of going to the eye hospital. The GP, although very sympathetic, told Dad he would contact the hospital, and whether he could drive or not was in their hands.

The thought of not being allowed to drive really upset Dad. His walking was very difficult with his right knee needing replacing. To be able to drive his car to the supermarket, and the High Street, was a must. He became very depressed and his tinnitus went into top gear. He was complaining of whistles and bangs in his ears, interspersed with the sound of steam trains. Sue was very concerned about him and contacted the GP about the depression and tinnitus. Dad made several visits and was put on anti-depressant pills, but they didn't work straight away.

Things were going from bad to worse, and it was on a Sunday afternoon when Sue received a phone call from Dad, pleading for help. There was a raging thunderstorm as she jumped in the car to drive to Dad's house. As she was holding the metal door handle of the car, her arm took quite a blow as the car was struck by lightning. All the electrics in the car were ruined, and she was very shaken. Still worried about Dad, she recovered herself, and her son took her to 'Franfay'.

Dad was in such a distressed state that she didn't want to leave him alone. She packed a bag with his help, and they took him back to her house. That evening he asked Sue if he could phone me. He didn't say much, just said he was suffering badly with the tinnitus, and he just wanted to hear my voice. I was obviously very worried, but grateful Sue had taken him to her house.

The next morning I woke at seven o'clock when the phone rang. It was Sue saying that Dad had taken some pills, and left a note beside the bed. It said, 'Please forgive me. I can't go on any longer.' Sue had tried to wake him, but with no success. She

113

thought he was breathing, so had phoned 999, and would phone me back. She phoned again in five minutes saying she had managed to wake Dad, and the ambulance was there. They were taking Dad to Southampton hospital, and she was going to follow in the car.

All day I waited for further news. Dad was very upset at waking, and was complaining bitterly about the noises in his head. The hospital established what tablets he had taken, and said he would be fine, he hadn't taken enough to do any lasting damage. They put him on a ward. On one side he had an elderly man coughing, and on the other side a man with a hissing machine which ran constantly. Dad was distraught at the noise. He was covering his ears, and saying, 'Get me out of here.' The next day the hospital arranged for Dad to have a visit from a psychiatric doctor, and her reaction was, 'We must get this poor man out from this noise. This isn't the place for him, I will make some arrangements.' Sue was then phoned and told there was a place for him in the Elderly Persons Unit at Barton-on-Sea. She was to collect him from Southampton and take him to Barton.

Sue duly took Dad out of the hospital and settled him in the car. She told him she was taking him to Barton, and started to drive away.

Dad thought about it, and said, 'I am not going to Barton, take me to your house.'

Sue said, 'I can't do that, Dad, you will find it far too noisy with the boys, and the dog barking.'

He then became very cross, and said if she tried to take him to Barton he would open the car door while they were going along, and jump out. In those days Sue only had an elderly car, and it didn't have central locking. She decided she would have to take him back to her house.

When they arrived she took Dad indoors and the phone started ringing, and dear old Monty, her boxer dog, started to bark and bark. Dad put his head in his hands and sobbed. How Sue persuaded him to get in the car and go to Barton was a miracle, but thanks to Monty he climbed into the car and stopped protesting.

The unit at Barton was peaceful and caring. Dad was welcomed, given a quiet room, tea and sympathy. The staff were not only caring with the patients, they showed great concern for the carers. Dad was seen by a doctor and given medication to calm him, and Sue was reassured he was in good hands, and she could visit the next day.

I had a real mother and father of a cold, with hot and cold flu symptoms, and I had been in bed for a couple of days feeling very rough. I was terribly worried about Dad and Sue, but I wasn't well enough to drop everything and dash to Hampshire. It was another four or five days before I could get myself together, and once again take Poppy down to 'Franfay'.

Sue took me to Barton, and Dad was pleased to see me, but feeling sheepish as he said, 'Whatever must you think of me?' It was so sad to see him in such a terrible state.

Sue and I had a meeting with Dr Walker at the Unit. He was wonderful with us, his quiet calm manner very reassuring and kindly. He told us the name of the anti-depressants he was giving Dad, but he said it would take time for them to have full effect. He didn't think Dad should really be living on his own, and he wanted us to think how we could arrange things differently. He envisaged Dad would be there for a few weeks, and he would keep us fully updated on progress.

We were very relieved Dad was in such good hands, and we had long chats about the way forward. The obvious solution to us was for Dad to move up to Leighton Buzzard and live with us. Dad had always wanted to be independent and not to be a burden upon us, but now, with the doctor saying what he had, we felt the time was coming for him to live in Leighton Buzzard. He had lived in 'Franfay' for over 50 years, and we were worried about uprooting him from Lymington, and his friends. (Amazingly, Dad never did have an issue with that.)

As Sue had taken all the responsibility for getting Dad into Barton, I took over the visiting from her while she took a break. Dad was still complaining bitterly about the noises in his head. He felt the tinnitus was the cause of his problems, and he became obsessed with wanting an ear, nose and throat surgeon to look at his ears. We discussed it with Dr Walker at Barton, and he said if we were willing to pay for a private appointment in one of the hospitals, he would be more than happy to let us take Dad out to the hospital for a consultation.

We found a surgeon who could see him at short notice at a hospital in Bournemouth, and Dad was very pleased we had made the arrangements. After Sue's experience with Dad threatening to jump out of the car, we were less than confident about the whole outing, but with both of us there we felt there was strength in numbers. Dad was much calmer on the medication, and came with us like a lamb.

The consultant looked at Sue and me as if we were mad when we explained the situation. He looked in Dad's ears, talked to him about tinnitus, and said plainly that there was nothing he could do to help. Poor Dad was really crestfallen, and as we helped him into the car he was looking tired and crumpled. We both wished we had never arranged the trip. Dad insisted we stop on the way back so that he could look at the sea, and have a cup of tea. He knew we always had a flask of tea available, but we were worried about the request to look at the sea. Looking was one thing, but we didn't want him jumping over the cliff! Sue parked as far away from the cliff top as possible, and we returned him to Barton safely.

The doctors were pleased with Dad's progress, but he insisted on spending most of his time sitting in the little garden at the Unit. The weather was warm, and he spent many hours in that garden. When I went to visit he would insist we both sit there, and I must admit it was very pleasant. He then started to ask the doctor if he could go home in the afternoons to 'Franfay', and just sit on the lawn and have a cup of tea. He only wanted an hour there each afternoon, and he was sure I would be happy to arrange it for him. The doctor agreed, and I was asked if I would do it. I was very apprehensive, but I knew I could rope in Sue as backup, so I agreed. He was thrilled to sit in his own garden each afternoon, and Poppy sat with him. He didn't play me up when I said we had to go, and the whole thing ticked along for a couple of weeks. Fortunately Barton wasn't too far away, as I seemed to be driving backwards and forwards constantly.

One particularly sunny day Sue phoned me and said she had baked a cake and would pop round with it that afternoon. I collected Dad and we all enjoyed sitting outside. When it was time for the return trip to Barton, Dad went into the kitchen, removed his sun hat, and said he was going to his desk to get some scissors. I followed him to his desk, he cut some sticky tape to put inside his hat, and handed me the scissors. I immediately went to put them out of harm's way, and we held an inquest into why Dad was putting sticky tape inside his hat. He made some remark about the label being scratchy, and it was now fine with tape over it. As long as he was happy, and he hadn't pocketed the scissors, we were OK with that. Sue left, and I took Dad back to Barton.

The next morning the Unit at Barton phoned me at eight o'clock in the morning. I was not to panic, but Dad was in

Bournemouth hospital. They had phoned for an ambulance as Dad had tried to slash his wrist. He was OK, he hadn't done lasting harm, but he needed proper dressings, and possibly stitches, so he was at the A&E department with one of their staff. I said I would drive over there immediately. I picked Sue up on the way, and we just couldn't fathom out what he could possibly have found that was sharp enough to cut his wrist.

Dad was once again very sheepish, and sorry for what he had done. We all knew it was another cry for help. Poor Dad was all bandaged, fully injected with antibiotics, and ready to return to Barton. Not knowing what the day was going to hold, I had put Poppy in the car, as I couldn't have left her shut in all day. My poor little blue 106 had to take Sue, myself, Dad, the member of staff from Barton, and Poppy, back along the Christchurch bypass. We were all like sardines in a tin, but we made it.

I was very worried that Dr Walker would refuse to take Dad back, but amazingly he did. I can't praise that Unit enough for the way they looked after us that day. 'Bring the dog in,' they said, and as we all trooped down the corridor I heard Dr Walker's colleague say, 'I must be losing the plot, I thought I saw a dog walk past my office!' Sue and I were both offered counselling, and we were all fed. Dad sat in the little lounge with us, as they had to transfer his belongings to another room. The carpet in his room was badly bloodstained, and would need professional cleaning. Dad kept saying he was sorry, and we asked him what he had used to cut his wrist. He confessed to removing a rusty old Stanley knife blade from his desk, and putting it in his pocket while we put the scissors away. At Barton he took his tube of toothpaste out of its box, and he hid the blade in the box.

The doctors decided that Dad needed a course of electrical

treatment to the head. It was called electroconvulsive therapy (ECT). At first Dad refused point-blank to have it, but one member of staff, a really nice motherly lady, managed to persuade him. It was arranged that he would be transferred to a specialist hospital in Southampton, and he would be there for at least a couple of weeks. Sue said she would hold the fort while I went home for a while, and so Poppy and I closed up 'Franfay' and headed for Leighton Buzzard.

I had talked through with John the possibility of moving Dad up to live with us, and it was good to sit round as a family and discuss what, if any, changes we would need to make. It would mainly be transferring Dad to a new doctor, and dentist, that sort of thing, as he had already been spending quite lengthy spells of time with us. His rooms were ready and waiting, and the plan was for me to bring Dad straight back from Southampton once he was well enough. I think it was rather more than a couple of weeks, but Poppy and I made the journey back to 'Franfay'.

The first afternoon I visited Dad, he was thrilled to see me. 'How on earth did you find me?' he said. 'I have been thinking of all the ways I could possibly contact you to let you know where I am. Where am I?' It was obvious Dad's memory of recent events had been erased, and he was very muddled and confused.

After the ninth treatment I saw a marked change in him, and on meeting Dr Walker from Barton I said, 'Dad is back.' He was very pleased with the information, but it was another three treatments before Dad was declared well enough to go home.

Sue and I attended a meeting at Barton, and we all discussed Dad's future, and his move to live with us. I was promised backup whenever I needed it, and they would contact the relevant professionals in Bedfordshire. It was a wet Wednesday when Poppy and I left 'Franfay' and made our way to Southampton. We picked up Dad, and drove the now very familiar route home.

Life had changed for Sue and myself while Dad had been away from 'Franfay'. I had realised the luxury of my little job had to go, because I was either in Lymington, or going to be looking after Dad full-time. It had been fun while it lasted. Sue, on the other hand, had been experiencing enormous changes in her life. Her husband had decided he wanted other things out of life, and announced he was leaving. It was a complete shock to Sue, who was left with two teenage boys, a boxer dog, several cats and a few elderly hens. She was running her own little business from home, and if the house had to be sold, and the proceeds divided, she would lose her only source of income. It was a very worrying time for her. We were all in a state of shock, and we weren't sure how Dad woud take the news. Fortunately she managed to secure a large loan on the house, and buy her husband out, so that she could still run her business and keep a roof over her family's head.

Dad was relieved to be out of hospital and not struggling to live alone. He never stopped saying how grateful he was to be living with family. He was still taking very high doses of medication, which Dr Walker had placed in my care. He was much calmer, but he was still complaining bitterly about the tinnitus.

One morning he came to me in the kitchen with one sleeve rolled up. He held his arm up, looked me straight in the eyes, and said, 'Will you tell me what these scars are all about?'

I couldn't lie to him, so I told him he was very ill when he was at the Unit in Barton, and the scars were the result of a cry for help.

'What did I use to do this?' he asked.

I had to confess it was a blade from a Stanley knife which he had smuggled in from his desk. He was very shaken about it for a while, but it was amazing to us how much memory he had lost. He never did remember about the overdose he took at Sue's house, and we never did tell him.

He insisted to the GP he wanted a specialist to look at his ears, and once again a consultant told him there was nothing that could be done. This doctor did say he would refer him to the Tinnitus Clinic at Milton Keynes hospital. That was a crumb of comfort. We made many visits to the hospital, and really patient people tried to explain to him he should not listen to the clatter of the tinnitus. He was given leaflets about white noise pillows, and quite a list of different possibilities for help. Unfortunately his loss of memory meant he could never quite remember all the advice he was given, no matter how many times we told him. He was convinced he had to have silence in his life, which we were told was completely the wrong approach to the problem.

He was referred for a hearing aid, and we duly went to all the appointments, but he just could not get to grips with the various kinds he tried. I made charts to show how he was to build up the wearing time, and I would hand out the hearing aid at the right times, but it didn't make any difference. Dad being a very stubborn person, we just didn't get anywhere with it. It was obvious he had been deaf for longer than we had appreciated, as he declared the birds were deafening, making all that noise. It was no good for his tinnitus.

For all the hospital appointments we were struggling with a folding wheelchair, which I had to take in the good old 106 car. Once I had removed it from the car and assembled it, I then had to push it, and Dad was quite a weight. Dad's right knee was getting too painful for sticks, even though the replacement left knee was good. He hated being pushed in a wheelchair, and he once again felt it was too much of a burden to put on me.

We can't remember which member of the family it was who suggested getting Dad a little folding mobility scooter that would go in the car. It may have been Dad's own suggestion, but what a can of worms that turned out to be. We took him to a mobility shop just outside Milton Keynes, and he saw a smart little three-wheeled red machine that said 'Zoom' on the front. He tried it out in the shop, we had demonstrations of how to take it apart and recharge the battery. The staff were very attentive, and Dad was like a child in a sweet shop. We came away with Dad's new toy – the little red Zoom. We all had high hopes of happy days out, with Dad able to ride his new machine while we walked alongside. Shopping trips, hospital appointments, holidays would all be made so much easier, we thought.

Before Dad was told his eyesight wasn't good enough for driving, Sue had taken him on a coach holiday to Scotland. He had really enjoyed it, and it must have seemed familiar to him after all the years of coach trips with Mum. Sue had enjoyed it too. In the evenings, when the elderly guests were being entertained, Sue would take her book and have a quiet drink in the bar. At that time Philip, the coach driver, would join her. They had long chats over drinks, and Philip was especially grateful to Sue for listening to all his troubles with his divorce. He was concerned about Dad's mobility getting on and off the coach. He helped him a lot, and became quite fond of Dad.

When Dad was finally settled with us in Leighton Buzzard Sue was visiting a friend, and made the acquaintance of another lady who was a medium. The friend, and the medium, invited her to join them for one of their meditation sessions. At this session the medium passed a message to Sue from Mum. She said, 'Your Mum is saying you must not be afraid to meet a man who will take you across the sea. He is a very good person, and you can trust him. He is being sent to help you.' Sue was surprised by the message. The last thing on her mind was getting involved with another man, and she certainly had no intention of going overseas.

Dad had been with us a few months when Sue phoned to say she had received a call from Philip, the coach driver, asking how Dad was getting on. She told him a lot of water had gone under the bridge since they were in Scotland. Her husband had gone, Dad had been in hospital, and was now living in Leighton Buzzard. Philip was shocked and suggested they meet for a coffee. Sue didn't feel she should do anything like that in case they were seen, and her divorce proceedings were affected. Philip then suggested they should meet up and have lunch in Yarmouth on the Isle of Wight. I think Sue could have been knocked to the ground with a feather. Mum's message, about 'don't be afraid to meet a man who will take you across the sea', suddenly became very significant.

Poppy had been having trouble with a front paw since leaving Lymington, and we had made quite a few visits to the vet. She had a scan, and we were all shocked to be told she had a nasty tumour. The vet gave her pills, and said she was fine for now, but we would know when the time was right to take any action. I was devastated. I knew she was eleven, but golden retrievers often live longer, and I wanted to give her as much enjoyment as we could.

In June that year Freddie had a week's holiday so we decided to book a log cabin in Tattershall, Lincolnshire. It was a part of the country that was new to us, and the journey wouldn't be too excruciatingly long. We decided to take two cars to Tattershall so that we could take four adults plus luggage, plus Poppy, and

Dad's pride and joy, his Zoom scooter. When we arrived we were pleased to see we were right beside a small shallow lake, and Poppy had good access to the edge to play her stone retrieving game. The weather was good and we all enjoyed seeing a different part of the country.

When we came home it became clear that Poppy was panting a lot with the steroid pills, and she wasn't looking happy. I booked an appointment with the vet, and I knew what she was going to say. I tried to prepare myself, but you never can. John came with me, and he couldn't bear to stay. I, on the other hand, had to be there for her, and stay with her while the vet put her to sleep. It is the most awful feeling when you walk out through the vet's door with your beloved pet's collar and lead in your hand, and no dog. I was so upset, I vowed I would never put myself through it again.

Mum's message through Ron kept running through my head. She had said there was a small dog with her. If Mum lived on, and had proved it to me, and mentioned our little dog, surely she must have Poppy with her. These thoughts should have been a comfort to me, but when you are grieving you are overtaken by emotion. We are all human beings, made up of emotions, and no matter how much we try to reason with ourselves we are compelled to grieve.

On returning from the vet we had to break the news to Dad. He was terribly upset. He had a great love of animals, and probably Sue and I love dogs so much because of Mum and Dad's influence when we were growing up. He went straight to his little sitting room, phoned Sue and sobbed his heart out down the phone. We tried our best to pick up the threads of normal life, but with one member of the family missing it is always difficult.

Dad took to riding his scooter along the pavements into town and round the shops. It wasn't something we had envisaged when we chose his scooter. We had focused on a model that would take apart easily, and fit into the back of the car. We had deliberately chosen it because it was light. Dad was quite a weight, and it wasn't long before he was trying to push it home because it had run out of charge. Various people, complete strangers, had been kindly helping him home, and I was starting to get anxious when he went out. We equipped him with a mobile phone, and stuck labels on it with the home telephone number. I was then getting calls to go to his aid. Finally the machine just wouldn't work, so we loaded it into the 106 and took it to the mobility shop. They took one look and saw that the axle was broken. They were very sorry, said it was still under guarantee, and gave him a bright new shiny machine.

Dad was overjoyed to have his wheels back again, and it wasn't long before he started to phone me from places like the canal towpath, saying the battery charge had run out. We had a real struggle to make him understand that he couldn't ride round and round for miles: he only had enough charge in the battery for the town and back. The penny dropped with us as to what was happening when a friend told me he had seen Dad 'off-roading'! We found Dad was coming home with the scooter covered in mud where he had been riding it through the fields. He told us he was finding the traffic noise too much for his ears, and the short cut down the riverside path, and across the field, was a much quieter route. Again it was only a matter of time before we were back at the mobility shop. Another broken axle was diagnosed, and he was given a lecture on not bumping it up and down kerbs. Amazingly, as we were still in the guarantee period, this second scooter was replaced. I can't believe how kind and tolerant they were at the shop. Dad was convinced his scooter riding was faultless, and the machines were rubbish.

The manager of the shop suggested, very tactfully, that maybe Dad would like a bigger, more robust model for riding around locally. The smaller take-apart model could then be kept for our out-of-town visits. Dad's eyes lit up at the prospect of a second scooter, and he wanted it immediately.

The bigger one was duly delivered to the house, and Dad was off down the road. This time the phone call came saying, 'I have got a puncture, and I am round the back of the Methodist church!' Fortunately it was a Saturday and John was at home, and we were able to recruit our next-door neighbour to help. The neighbour had a truck, and between John, Freddie and Allan they had enough manpower to lift the scooter into the truck. It was obvious that punctures were going to be a hazard we could do without, so much to Dad's disgust the mobility shop delivered and fitted a set of solid tyres.

Still missing Poppy, I decided to go along to the Spiritualist meeting one Wednesday evening. The visiting medium asked if she could give me a message, and I readily agreed. It was from Mum. She said she had my dog. She also had the little dog from my childhood, and this little one had taught Poppy how to come and visit me. She said they were giving her a hard time because she kept losing them. Each time, she found they were visiting me, and she had to explain to Poppy that she could visit now and again, but not all the time. She also said I was worrying about Dad when he went out. She said I was to stop worrying because she would look after him when he was out on his own.

I was delighted with this message. I couldn't figure out the rules of the Spirit World, but I took it to mean they had to live their lives in the Spirit World more than here. They were only allowed visiting rights. It was wonderful to hear that Mum had Poppy. I had hoped she was looking after her, but it was a marvellous comfort for me to be told this by a complete stranger, who knew nothing about me, or my life. It was quite an eye-opener that Mum was able to reason with the dogs. Thank goodness she was keeping an eye on Dad, as he was beginning to be quite a handful at the age of 87.

He had been having great difficulty getting in and out of the bath, and we decided he needed a proper bath lifter. I made an appointment for us to visit the Disability Resource Centre, not too far from Leighton Buzzard. We were taken round their displays of equipment by a fully qualified physiotherapist, which was such a help. She explained the merits of all the different styles, and types of lifter. Dad was full of himself that day, laughing and joking, and telling the poor long-suffering physio that all he needed was a rope ladder. Luckily she was able to see the funny side of it, but it was hard to get Dad to be sensible. He finally said he wanted a lifter that would sit flat on the bottom of the bath. A sort of large strap that was slowly lowered by a motor fixed to the wall.

The physio was very much against the idea on the grounds of safety, and explained the merits of a contraption that stood in the bath permanently. We left, having decided on the sensible option, and the physio wished me luck with Dad, as she could see I was going to need it. The lifter was delivered and installed in the bath. Dad moaned continually that he was not sitting low enough in the water, and wasn't getting a good bath. We felt that at least it was safe, and we would just have to put up with Dad's complaints.

In the mornings it was always my practice to sit Dad at the dining room table with his breakfast and the newspaper, while I went into his bathroom to clean. As I entered the bathroom I could not believe my eyes. I just stood staring. There was a hole in the side of the bath the size of a dinner plate! It wasn't low down, it was up towards the top of the bath.

I dashed into the dining room and said to Dad, 'What has happened to the bath?' He looked at me in disbelief when I told him there was a huge hole in it. We hurried into the bathroom and Dad was genuinely shocked. He admitted he had been a bit wobbly when he was drying himself, and had grabbed hold of the back of the lifter. He had pulled it towards him, and then let it go. The result was that it smashed a hole in the bath, but Dad hadn't noticed.

It was quite a nuisance as far as Dad was concerned as he didn't like using the shower, and we didn't think he was steady enough on his feet to use it on his own. From then on we employed a carer to come in and help Dad in the mornings. We also called in the services of Harry and Dan, our plumbing handymen. They could not stop laughing at the size of the hole in the bath, but they set to work installing a new bath, and retiling. Dad insisted he was not going to use the bath lifter that, in his words, had 'caused the problem', ever again. We gave in, and ordered the much more dicey strap system, and he loved it.

10

The Zoom Basher

Dad had regular visits to the GP to check his blood pressure and heart condition, and to see he was fine taking the mountain of pills he was given each day. At one of these regular visits the GP commented on how bad Dad's knee was looking. It was starting to stick out at an angle. She encouraged Dad to go to see a consultant, and he agreed. When the consultant saw the X-rays he was quite alarmed. He told Dad his kneecap was in danger of slipping, and if that happened, there was nothing that could be done. Dad would have a stiff leg for the rest of his life. He told Dad he would put him on his emergency list for a replacement knee, and poor old Dad knew he had to face going into hospital again for more surgery. I knew he felt at his age that he couldn't be doing with it all, but he didn't have much choice if he didn't want a stiff leg. He just wanted to enjoy himself riding around on his scooter.

Sue came to stay for a few days and we were able to visit Dad in the hospital together. This time all went well, and he was home within a week. He was managing with his sticks, and refused to use a walking frame. He was, however, having difficulty getting out of his chair. Once more we visited the mobility shop for him to equip himself with a motorised rise and recline chair. The staff in the shop had begun to know Dad by this time, and when we went to purchase the chair we found out that Dad had a nickname at the shop. He was affectionately known to them as 'the Zoom Basher' as he had smashed up so many scooters!

Freddie was still working hard at the supermarket, and I sometimes felt very sorry for him living with us oldies, in what was beginning to look like an old folks' home. He never complained, and was always ready to help Dad with anything he could. When he first returned home from boarding school I persuaded him to go on a long weekend break to Center Parcs. It was arranged by AFASIC for their members over the age of 18, and they organised it with plenty of link leaders. Freddie, being quiet and shy, wasn't too sure about spending a weekend with a group of strangers, but he thought about it, and decided perhaps he would try it. The boarding schools had given him confidence, and I was thrilled that he was willing to go.

From what he managed to tell us on his return, we thought he had stayed in a bungalow with several AFASIC members, and his leaders were a student doctor and a student speech therapist. He had a wonderful time. It was one occasion when he showed emotion, when AFASIC announced they couldn't arrange any further trips as their funding had been withdrawn. Freddie commented, 'If it's good don't do it again.' Surprisingly shortly after this announcement from AFASIC, we received a phone call from the father of one of the young people who had been to Center Parcs. He asked if Freddie would be interested in going on a bunkhouse holiday, if he could find enough people to go. He had been talking to a couple who had been link leaders for AFASIC. They were willing to lead a holiday. Freddie was delighted to hear this, and out of it came a wonderful week in the Yorkshire Dales. He returned home from that week really excited. The whole thing had been a huge success, and the leaders were looking into planning another week the following year.

Dad's house, 'Franfay', had been rented out when he decided to move in with us. Sue had kept an eye on things as she was near, and the agents had found tenants. On hearing that the second set of tenants were moving out, Dad decided he wanted to sell 'Franfay'. We were all rather surprised by his decision, as we thought it might be too upsetting for him to part with his happy family home. He had lived in it for over 50 years. He was adamant, so when the tenants moved out, Sue went in to inspect the property. It was all looking very sad. We had specified in the rental agreement that 'no exotic pets' were allowed. Being animal lovers, we didn't want to stop a family having a dog or cat. What Sue found to her horror was that the tenants had kept a pet squirrel in the house. It had chewed its way through the cables to Dad's favourite bath lifter, and I think that made Dad's mind up that he wanted to sell the house.

In my experience life has a habit of giving you the ups, and the downs always seem to follow. We were relieved that after the break-up of her marriage Sue had got together with Philip, and they were very happy together. Philip helped Sue clear the garage of all Dad's tools, and all the items that needed removing before a sale. He worked tirelessly, ferrying stuff around in his elderly Land Rover. Sue could never have managed it all on her own.

It was the most almighty shock to all of us when Philip suddenly dropped dead in front of Sue. They had been together for 18 months. The first I heard was a tearful phone call from Sue's eldest son's girlfriend. She said, 'The ambulance has been, and they have taken Philip to hospital. Sue has gone with them, but Auntie Wendy, I know he is dead.' I could not believe that Sue was going to be left on her own again.

Philip was divorced and had grown-up children, so of course Sue had to contact them and break the news. The children, as family, had the task of organising the funeral, but they told Sue that Philip was happier when he was with her than they had ever known him. They wanted him buried in the local cemetery, with a service in the local church, and Sue was put in charge of the arrangements. She had been having a discussion about Scotland with him in the pub, only a few weeks before his death. Philip had spent quite some time there, taking his coach parties up there and back. He told Sue how he had grown to love the sound of the bagpipes in their outdoor setting. He then added that when he died he would like a lone piper playing at the graveside.

Sue finally finished arranging the funeral, discussing and making decisions with Philip's family. I really believe the only thing that carried her along at the time was Mum's secret code, and the fact she knew in her heart that Philip lived on. John took some time off work to look after Dad, and the household in Leighton Buzzard, while I went down to Lymington to be with Sue for the funeral. As we left Sue's house in the funeral car, and slowly approached the church, the distant sound of the bagpipes, getting slightly louder and louder as we drew close, was just so magical and emotional. I held Sue's hand very tightly as we entered the church, which was packed with Philip's friends, family and work colleagues. I whispered to Sue that Philip was quite likely with us, watching everything. Through her tears and sorrow, she kept composed, and I was very proud of her because I knew how much she was really hurting inside.

As part of the funeral party we followed the coffin in the cars. As we approached the cemetery again we heard the strains of the bagpipes. The piper was stood at the graveside, and the music gently blowing in the wind was so beautiful. When the coffin had been lowered, and the vicar had sympathised with the mourners, the undertaker gently asked if the family were ready to get back into the cars. Philip's ex-wife said 'Yes', and everyone started to walk to the cars. The grave was just one little empty plot in the midst of lots of graves that had been there for many years.

What shook me was the fact it was so close to Mum's grave. Sue stepped into the funeral car, and sat quietly looking at Philip's grave on one side of the path, and Mum's on the other side. We were then treated to an unexpected scene of wailing, and yelling, from Philip's ex-wife who had run back to the grave-side. Her children gathered round her, and gently tried to pull her away and persuade her to get in the car. I couldn't believe my eyes; there was Sue looking so alone, sitting in the car between the two graves that meant so much to her. There at the grave-side was the wailing. I knew where Philip was, and it wasn't at the grave.

I hated leaving Sue and returning to Leighton Buzzard, but I knew her son and his girlfriend were staying in the house with her. All her friends would rally round, and she assured me she was fine.

I hadn't been home for many weeks before Sue phoned to say her friend, the medium, had been round. Philip had come through to her. She said to Sue, 'He is saying you two had been together in an earlier life. When you met it was obvious you both knew one another well.' Sue confirmed this was very true. The medium said, 'When you were together before, you were in Rome.' Sue was amazed at this as Philip had kept saying to her, 'I really want to take you to Rome.' The medium also said it was never intended for him to stay long. Sue told me she always believed Philip was only going to be with her a short time.

Dad didn't know what to make of the fact that Sue's husband had left her, and then she had another man living with her who she called her partner. In Dad's old eyes you were either married or you weren't!

Dad was still terrorising the town on his daily jaunts through the fields, and goodness knows where, on his big scooter. When he complained about his glasses I seized the opportunity to get him an optician's appointment. I knew the optician in Lymington had said his cataracts needed doing, and I was expecting trouble. I took him to see my optician, a gentleman well respected in the town, and someone I knew I could trust.

I went into the eye test room with Dad, and I was horrified when Dad's opening gambit was, 'I can see perfectly well, and I have no intention of having my cataracts corrected.'

I could tell the poor optician had taken a big intake of breath before he had started the test. When it was complete he spoke to Dad very kindly, and told him his cataracts were more than ready for attention, but nobody could force him to do things against his will. He told Dad that the longer he left it, the harder it would be to give him good eyesight again, and if left, he would eventually go blind. Dad just reiterated the fact that he could see perfectly well, and the optician, banking on the fact Dad's ears were as bad as his eyes, quietly muttered in my direction, 'I doubt that.'

Before Dad could forget what the optician had said, I had a serious chat with him about how he would cope when he was blind. It made him think hard, and eventually he agreed to ask the GP to get him an appointment at the eye hospital. We duly turned up at Milton Keynes hospital with Dad riding his little red Zoom, and we saw a lady doctor. As soon as the poor lady entered the room Dad was complaining bitterly to her about the floaters in his eyes.

She gave his eyes a good examination, and then said, 'Your cataracts do need doing, but I am not willing to put you on the waiting list, as there is nothing that can be done about the floaters. If we do your cataracts, you will be back here complaining to me that the floaters are a problem.' She then walked out of the room.

Dad then rounded on me saying, 'There you are, my cataracts don't need doing', and he was thrilled with himself because he had put a stop to that little idea.

Time passed, and once again Dad started to complain about his glasses being no good. Back we went to see the long-suffering optician, and once again he said he would write to the GP about sending him to the eye hospital. This time the doctor sent him to Stoke Mandeville Eye Unit. Once again we entered with Dad on his, by this time, rather battered red Zoom. I was impressed with the organisation there: first Dad saw a nurse for a chat, then an eye test, and his file was put in a pile ready for the doctor.

When Dad's name was called it was by Mr Jones, who was the head of the department. He was very good with Dad, and explained all about floaters, cataracts and the working of the eyes. I could tell Dad was impressed, and when he told Dad his right cataract was so bad he would have to have a general anaesthetic to remove it, Dad was quite shocked. He agreed meekly, and I was amazed.

Six weeks later I took Dad to Stoke Mandeville with his little bag. Again it was all very slick, and Mr Jones came to talk to me while Dad was in recovery. It had been an extremely difficult operation, but he felt it would really improve Dad's sight. There had unfortunately been a small bleed at the back of Dad's eye, nothing serious, but it would take a few weeks to clear, and would obstruct Dad's vision while it was clearing.

135

I sat beside Dad's bed in a little bay of six people, and Dad was very restless. After he came round he kept asking me the same questions over and over again. I had quite a struggle to keep him in the bed. By early evening the nurse ordered me out, and I promised to return at 7.30 the next morning, as I suspected he was going to cause trouble.

The next day as I walked in I could see Dad sitting on a chair in a communal area, and he was crying. I went up to him and he said, 'They have made me leave my bed, and I couldn't find the breakfast room.' He had wound himself up into an emotional state, and the disorientation was back.

Back at home, as the anaesthetic wore off, he became more aware of his eyes, and was extremely distressed about the black 'spiders', as he called them, in his eye. I was putting his drops in for him several times a day, but he was convinced his eyesight had been ruined. He ranted and raved, and insisted upon staying in a darkened room. The hospital advised I should not let him stay in the dark, and he would be fine in a few weeks. They were very difficult weeks. Dad was on a high dose of anti-depressant pills, but he was very angry. At one stage he made us put a clothes rack in front of the television with a sheet on it. We never did fathom out what that was all about. We also had an incident when he was lying on his bed telling us to send for the undertakers! He was so upset about not being able to go out on his scooter that I devised a plan whereby he would wear his big wrap-around sunglasses, and sit on his little scooter. I would walk beside him and steer the scooter round the block. Once out in the daylight, he wanted extra protection for his eyes. He made me put sticking plasters down the sides of his glasses. He looked like a comical racehorse with blinkers!

It was scary for us, after everything that had happened at the Unit in Barton. When he left there they had promised me backup in Bedfordshire, so I decided to call for my backup, and I took Dad to see a doctor at the Elderly Persons Unit in Houghton Regis, not far from us. The doctor was very kind to Dad, spoke to him nicely, and carried out a standard memory test. He was very concerned that at such a great age, and in Dad's circumstances, he had undergone a general anaesthetic. He explained how confused elderly people can become, and made it obvious to me that dementia had really set in. He knew the eye hospital were hoping to sort out Dad's other cataract when the first eye would allow, and he didn't want Dad to have another general anaesthetic. He persuaded Dad he didn't want one, and he wrote to Mr Jones, telling him Dad had requested a local anaesthetic for the second eye operation.

The appointment was made for Dad's second cataract operation. A couple of weeks before that, I had to take Dad to see the heart specialist. Dad had suffered several heart attacks in middle age, and he had been on heart medication ever since. The specialist carried out a scan, and said he thought it would be a good idea to increase Dad's medication. He could see Dad's high doses of anti-depressants in his list of medicines, and put him on some different tablets for his heart. That didn't really mean anything to Dad, I was the one who sat for a couple of hours every four weeks counting out all his pills, and putting them into boxes for the days of the week, and the time of day.

The new medication started, and Dad suddenly began to complain of pains on the top of his head. I took him to see the GP. It wasn't our regular doctor, we saw somebody else, and he said Dad had sunburn. It didn't really ring true to me, but Dad did have a very healthy-looking brown tan from all his scooter riding. I put cream on Dad's head and still Dad complained. In the end I took him back to see the same GP. I could see some dark red blotches, and it looked to me like shingles. Again the doctor said it was sunburn. I pointed out the blotches and asked if Dad could possibly have shingles. At this the doctor became quite cross, and confirmed again it was sunburn.

Dad's cataract appointment was the following day, and in the night Dad pressed his emergency bell which rang beside my bed. I went downstairs and found Dad in tears, and in absolute agony with his head. I made him a cup of tea, and gave him some painkillers. I phoned the eye hospital to let them know we would not be coming. I lay awake, wondering what I should do next. I had a quiet word with Mum in my head, and said, 'Please point me in the right direction with this.'

As soon as the heart surgeon's office was open, I phoned and explained. I wanted to know if Dad's new pills could be causing the problem. Within a couple of hours the heart surgeon himself was on the phone. He couldn't diagnose over the phone, but it sounded like shingles to him. I was astounded he had said what I had been thinking. I relayed my conversations with the GP and said I didn't know what to do, or where to turn.

He said, 'You take him straight to the A&E department at the hospital, and use my name. Say I want him seen.'

I told poor old Dad that we were off to the A&E department at the hospital, and he was convinced by this time that he had a growth on his head. When we arrived I explained to the receptionist, who promptly told us it was a GP matter. I informed her of the heart specialist's instruction and she relented, telling us to 'Sit down', in an angry tone.

When Dad's turn came, some hours later, a doctor who looked no more than 12 years old called us in. She was a sweet girl who looked straight at Dad's head and said, 'You have shingles.' Thanks to the GP, Dad was too late for the tablets, so the young doctor gave me some sachets of light anaesthetic, the kind they put on children's hands before an injection. Dad suffered badly, and having had shingles myself I felt very sorry for him.

Weeks later, with fear and trepidation I took Dad to the hospital for the second cataract removal. His first eye was now much better, and although Dad would not say how good it was when the blood cleared, we knew he was much calmer. The second time around, everything worked like clockwork. Dad didn't have to stay in hospital overnight, and he didn't complain. Within a week we could tell his eyesight was much better. Dad was back to his old tricks on his scooter, which was gradually looking rather a wreck.

Once he could see the state of his precious big scooter, he decided he would carry out some repairs. Throughout his life he had always been keen on 'do it yourself'. He had built a bay-windowed single-storey extension on to the kitchen at 'Franfay', and thankfully had a friend who was a builder. When the friend questioned him about how he had supported the bathroom above, the friend suggested they hurry round to the house together, before the bathroom fell into the kitchen. Dad had also decided to instal central heating into the house, shortly before our wedding. My Mum was not amused as on the day guests were expected he still had floorboards up in the bedrooms.

He decided a can of spray paint, such as you use on cars, would be ideal for a quick respray of the mudguards on his scooter. He had always been slightly colour blind, and the colour was not a good match. It provided him with hours of fun, but we learnt when he put his painting trousers on it was time to move our car out of the drive. We also put sheets of polythene down in the middle of the car port, and placed his scooter on them. That way it saved the drive, and the brickwork of the house, from being covered in paint when the wind blew. He was never 100 per cent satisfied with his modifications to the scooter, and sprayed and resprayed, probably for the fun of it.

Such was his obsession with his scooter that after his second knee replacement he didn't walk as much as he should have done. We tried to explain to him that he could park his scooter outside a shop, remove the key, and walk into the shop. That didn't suit; he was always convinced thieves were waiting to take his scooter the minute he left it. When he set off for town he would always ask me if there was any shopping I wanted. I knew it was useless asking him as he always forgot, but on one occasion I asked him if he could pop into the chemist for something. I was aghast when he told me he couldn't. 'The woman in there is a sourpuss,' he said, 'and she has banned me from the shop.' I didn't dare enquire why!

11

Mishaps

Freddie went to Yorkshire for his, now annual, group holiday in the Dales, and John and I took the opportunity to take Dad to the Lake District for the week. The Lakes had been another favourite for Mum and Dad in their coach trip days, so Dad was keen to see the area again. We had been there a few days, and the weather was being kind, so we packed the red Zoom, and set off for Keswick for the day. Dad decided a boat trip on the lake would be a good idea. It took about an hour to get there, so we bought our tickets for the boat trip, and made plans to find a little vegetarian restaurant that was recommended in a guide book. All was going well, but parking in July, in Keswick, was a nightmare. Eventually we decided to park in the supermarket car park, and go inside to buy a few items. John was always keen to buy a newspaper, so Dad said he was quite happy in the car for a short while. I took a basket and collected what I needed, and waited in the checkout queue. I duly put my shopping on the moving band and stood patiently. As the lady in front of me moved forward a huge bottle of olive oil, that was part of her shopping, toppled over, hit the side of the band, and smashed into tiny pieces, all over my trousers. I was just frozen to the spot with shock and disbelief. One trouser leg was completely soaked in oil all the way down, and my shoes were both soaked. I was left standing in a large puddle of broken glass and oil.

The lady in front of me screamed with horror, and was absolutely mortified at what she had done to me. She couldn't stop saying how sorry she was, and I was just standing motionless, because I was afraid of slipping on the oil. John, who had been standing waiting for me, rushed over and said, 'Are you all right?' The check-out lady pressed her bell for a supervisor, and she came with a big roll of white paper. Holding onto the side of the check-out I carefully took my feet out of my shoes, and tried not to stand on the broken glass. The supervisor mopped furiously with her paper, and handed me a piece. I paid for my shopping, and John packed it and took it to the car. I was left standing there still dripping, no shoes on, just holding a greasy pair of shoes and a length of paper in my hand.

My mind was racing, thinking what on earth I should do. I couldn't get into the car, it would put oil over the seat. I couldn't go into a shop and buy any old trousers, because I would drip all over their premises. We were an hour away from base, we had tickets for the boat trip on the lake that afternoon, and Dad and John were sitting in the car waiting to go and get lunch. I asked the check-out lady where the toilets were, and fortunately it was a big enough store to have them. I padded my dripping oily way to the Ladies. Once in there, I washed my shoes in soap and water, and dried them with the paper I had been given. I went into a cubicle and took off my trousers. As soon as it was quiet I tiptoed out, and filled a basin with hot soapy water. I dipped the offending trouser leg into the water, and proceeded to scrub as much of the oil out as possible. I was dearly hoping nobody would come through the door and see me standing there in my knickers. Murphy's law dictated that they weren't my best knickers of course. Suddenly the door flew open, and a whole queue of ladies came through the door. Their coach had parked so they could have a 'comfort stop'! They were a jolly bunch, and I tried to explain what I was doing. All they said was, 'Oh yes, fine story.' I don't think I have ever felt so embarrassed.

I continued to wash my trousers, and when the hand dryers finally fell silent it was my turn to attempt to dry my washing. I finally left the Ladies with sticky-feeling shoes, and wearing trousers with one wet leg.

John just said, 'Don't worry, we are near Derwent Water, people will think you fell in the lake.' He had assembled the Zoom, and with Dad riding beside us, we set off for the veggie restaurant. My luck was in, they had tables outside, and the sun was shining. I sat myself with my leg in the sun, and my thick wet trouser leg soon began to return to the same cream colour as the other one.

While we were in the area, Dad was keen to meet up with one of my Mum's cousins. Douglas is a jolly character, and he had lived with Mum and Dad when I was very young. They had been living in Surrey at the time, and Douglas was a student at the London School of Economics. He had spent his working life in Yorkshire, where he still lives with his wife, his family now being grown up and having children of their own. We arranged a lunchtime gathering, and it wasn't long before we were all laughing about the old family stories. It was good to see Dad enjoying himself, and we decided to take some photographs. Douglas produced his camera, and then he warned us about clipping the camera case to your belt. He had been doing that for some time, and whilst on holiday he stopped at a service area to use the loo. As he was standing at the loo his camera slipped off his belt and fell in. It was an expensive camera, and he hadn't had it long. He had to plunge his hand down the toilet to retrieve it, then wash it, and his hands, thoroughly. Needless to say the camera didn't work, and he had to take it back to the shop for repair. The shop asked what had happened to the camera, and he didn't have the heart to tell them the truth. He just said it had fallen into a bucket of water. It cost him over £200 for the repair. The most expensive penny he had ever spent!

We collected Freddie from the bunkhouse at the end of his week's holiday, and he had enjoyed another wonderful week. The leaders were looking exhausted as they carried the remaining sacks of potatoes to the minibus, but still saying they would be doing another holiday the next year.

When we returned to Leighton Buzzard we found our lawn looking as if someone had come in with a rotavator. It was just a mass of torn-up grass, with deep holes. We looked over the fences at the neighbours' gardens, and they had immaculate lawns. On closer inspection we had to conclude we had received a visit from some wild animal. It was puzzling, as the fences looked intact, and we couldn't find any gaps. John set to work to pick up all the dead grass, and fill in the holes. Within a few days it had happened again. Still the neighbours' gardens were fine.

John decided to call in a pest control man. He inspected the holes and declared that in his opinion it was either a badger or a fox. The way to find out was to put apples around at night time, and see if the following morning they had been nibbled. If they had, it would be badgers. If not, we were to try putting a chicken out on the lawn, and if that went, it would be a fox. We started with the apples, and left them out for a week, but nothing and nobody touched them. I went to the supermarket and bought a frozen chicken. I felt really stupid unwrapping this chicken and sitting it on the lawn before I went to bed, especially as I am vegetarian! Again, the chicken obviously didn't appeal to Mr Fox, but we always wondered whether a chicken with feathers would have been more appealing than a frozen supermarket specimen. The holes still appear in spring and autumn, but not to the extent they did. We still can't work out what digs the holes, which seem too deep for squirrels, nor how those who dig, get in. We have decided we must have badgers with parachutes.

We have often said that Leighton Buzzard must be a magnet for strange happenings in gardens. My friend, the manager of the office where I worked for a few months, woke up one morning to find the most beautiful, immaculate, pyramids of fallen apples in her garden. They were also in a neighbour's garden. They had lots of fallen apples around at the time, and they just couldn't understand why anyone would come in the night, and spend time building such beautiful pyramids. They checked the locks on their rear gates, all was secure, and they couldn't find a point of entry, or any signs of anyone having been around.

It remained a mystery for quite a long time, until my friend met a lady who was a medium. She told her the pyramids had been built by the Spirit World, to break up some lines of very bad energy that were running through their property. My friend's daughter had suffered with leukaemia, and the young girl next door had been very ill. The medium said the lines had run through the sleeping areas of the two girls, and out through the gardens. Dowsing for geopathic stress was carried out, and the energy lines pegged. There has, to my knowledge, been no trouble since.

Dad now had fairly good eyesight, but the problems with his hearing were getting worse, and the tinnitus still bothered him. In the summer, out and about on his scooter, he was always happier than in winter. If he couldn't go out he became depressed very quickly. Sue decided I needed a break, so she suggested he stay with her for a couple of weeks. She thought it would be good for her sons to spend time with their grandfather again. We had delivered Dad, complete with his travelling scooter, and Sue had quite a few ideas for places he might like to visit.

Unfortunately she hadn't experienced Dad's outings on the scooter, and one of her first suggestions was a visit to the Saturday market in Lymington High Street. It had always been a busy market, with stalls down either side of the main shopping area. It is popular with locals and tourists alike, and the pavements become quite crowded. The Zoom had a very good speed control, but Dad considered it something you didn't bother about. He set it to full speed, and as far as he was concerned, why would you need anything else? Sue and Dad hadn't gone very far down the pavement when the arm-rest on the scooter became hooked into the sleeve of a lady's coat. The poor woman found herself being propelled at speed, and people were all staring as she screamed, and yelled at Dad to stop. He couldn't hear her, and he just kept going. Poor Sue had to sprint through the people to haul him to a standstill. He was completely unaware of what he had done. Sue apologised profusely to the lady, who on inspection wasn't injured, just very shaken. Dad really couldn't understand what all the fuss was about, and Sue had her first taste of my life in Leighton Buzzard.

When he returned from Lymington, it wasn't long before his ninetieth birthday. As a family we all had discussions about how to mark the occasion. For his eighty-ninth we had taken him on a canal boat trip on a Sunday lunchtime. Sue, her sons, and various members of the family had all joined us for a roast lunch, served on the canal boat. We thought Dad would love it, but a young couple with a baby also joined the trip, and the baby screamed from the time they boarded the boat until they disembarked. It was very embarrassing for them, they tried all kinds of ways to quieten the baby, but there was nothing they could do. We felt very sorry for them, but for Dad it was a bad experience, as he said it had sent his tinnitus into overdrive.

Anxious not to get into any such situations again, we decided on a two-part treat for him. The first was a surprise lunch at home, on his birthday. As his bedroom adjoined the dining room, his entrance was straight out of his bedroom door. The night before his birthday, when he was safely in his room, and in bed, we quietly set up extra tables and chairs in the dining room, and decorated with balloons. We made the tables look pretty, and hung banners saying 'Happy 90th Birthday' around the walls. When he came out of his room the next morning he gasped, and said, 'Oh no, what are you planning?' In fact he had a wonderful time, as we had invited all his relatives who lived within striking distance, and Sue made the journey up from Lymington. Dad told all his old stories, and out came the photograph album.

The second part of his treat was a short break at Center Parcs, Longleat. John, Freddie and I figured it would be safe for him to ride his scooter around the forest and the bungalows, free from traffic. We hired bicycles, and we had great plans for all riding around together. We had a little bungalow that had its entrance via a path through the trees, and it was up a fairly steep slope. Dad, with his usual enthusiasm, took a run at the path with his scooter on full throttle, and tried to do a 'wheelie' round the corner. The result was that he fell into the undergrowth between the trees one way, and his scooter fell back down the path the other way. We all ran to Dad, horrified, wondering how

147

many limbs he had broken. He just stood up, dusted himself down, and was more concerned where his Zoom had gone. We took him into the bungalow and sat him down, and I made lunch.

We were all sitting round enjoying our meal when there was a knock at the door. A gentleman was standing there with a black bag, and introduced himself as a doctor. He said the passing Disability Bus driver had reported seeing an elderly man rolling around under the trees. He had come to check, and see what it was all about. Dad was most indignant, and said there was nothing wrong with him. The doctor insisted on giving Dad a check-over, and had to admit he seemed in remarkable shape for someone celebrating his ninetieth birthday.

The following day we decided to keep Dad away from more scooter antics in the woods, so we took him to the Safari Park. He immediately saw the car racing simulator, and enquired if we were all going inside.

I looked at the cabin-type arrangement that housed it, and saw how it tipped from side to side. 'I am not going in that,' I said.

John said, 'Neither am I.'

Dad looked disappointed and said to Freddie, 'Well, you will come in with me, won't you?' Freddie agreed, and in they went. John mentioned to the man on the door that Dad was 90, and he said, 'Well he must be quite the oldest person we have ever had in here'.

When they came out, Freddie was grinning, and Dad said in a very loud voice, 'Not as good as others I have been in'!

A friend in Leighton Buzzard asked if I would take her to a Spiritualist meeting, so shortly after returning from Longleat I took her along. I think she was quite surprised at the informal atmosphere, and the friendliness. We had a good visiting medium, and after giving several people messages, she asked if she could come to me. She told me she had a lady in the Spirit World who had died in her sleep. She felt it was a work colleague of mine. I was really surprised. I only knew one person who had died in her sleep, and I had worked with her in the shipping solicitors office in London. It was dear old Cassie, as we called her, the one who had oiled the doll's eye switchboard. The girls from the office had told me when she died, and how she had gone to bed and just not woken up. I was quite upset at the time as I had been talking to her on the phone not many weeks before. I was trying to arrange a reunion, and Cassie was very excited at the prospect of meeting again. I cancelled the plans for the reunion, and we didn't get it together after that. Cassie just wanted to say hello to me, let me know she was all right, and to tell me she thought I had turned out very well. I was very touched, and thrilled to think she had gone to the trouble of making contact. I was sorry my friend didn't receive a message, but I think the whole procedure was very strange to her. She was just content to look and listen, and take it all in.

Dad was delighting in telling everyone he was 90. He was very proud of the fact. But one evening after dinner he started to have severe pains in his tummy. I phoned for the out-of-hours doctor, who came an hour or so later. Dad was lying on his bed in great discomfort. After checking him over, the doctor phoned for an ambulance. I hastily packed a few items in a bag, and I travelled in the ambulance with Dad. John followed us to Stoke Mandeville hospital in the car. Once at the hospital Dad was given blood tests, and X-rays, and we waited around for what seemed an age, until he was taken to a ward, and settled in a bed. As by this time it was about 2 a.m. I was told to go home, and come back the following morning with Dad's razor and

149

washing bag. We were very worried that Dad had just reached 90, and now things were going wrong. We fell into bed exhausted, and I was up early the next morning.

As soon as I had dropped Freddie at work I headed for Stoke Mandeville. I went into Dad's ward, and found him in bed making terrible moaning noises. A nurse came along and told me to leave, as visiting time wasn't until the afternoon. I explained I had been asked to come back to bring Dad's toiletries. She left, and I stayed a little longer with Dad. All the nurses seemed to disappear, and then a doctor came in, walking straight up to Dad's bed.

He asked if I was a relative, and I explained I was Dad's daughter, and carer. He took lots of information from me about Dad, and asked if I had any help from outside the family. I said, 'No, I look after him myself.' He said he was most impressed, and asked me more questions. He looked around for a nurse to help him take some blood from Dad, but there were no nurses to be found. He looked at me and asked if I would be prepared to hold Dad's arm, and help him. I didn't mind at all. He told me Dad was going to be taken for a scan very soon. In fact, after the doctor left, two nurses returned with a trolley, and I was ordered out.

It was a very worrying time, I didn't know what was happening. But when I returned from my afternoon visit to the hospital, I received a phone call almost straight away. It was the charming doctor who had spoken to me in the morning. He said he just wanted me to know that Dad had been moved to another ward, and gave me the number. He didn't want me visiting and finding Dad wasn't in his previous place. He may have said he was impressed with me, but I was impressed with him, taking the trouble to phone me. The next afternoon I found the appropriate ward, and Dad was sitting on the bed looking like thunder.

He looked at me and said, 'I am surprised you have shown your face.'

I was shocked. I said, 'Dad, whatever do you mean?'

He said, 'John brought me in here last night, and you have both dumped me here to die.'

I gasped, and said something like, 'Don't ever be so silly.'

I sat on the bed with him, and a passing nurse scowled at me and said, 'A bit of straight talking to him wouldn't go amiss.'

I was beginning to wonder what on earth had been going on. Dad wanted to get back into the bed, and said he wanted the curtains drawn round the bed. I did as I was told, and sat with him inside the curtains.

The lady in the next bed, not realising I was in there, started to regale her visitors with the tales of the day. 'We had a big scene in here today,' she said. 'The old chap in the bed next door shouted at the doctors when they came on their rounds. He told them he knew his rights, they couldn't keep him here against his will. The doctors stood and stared at him, then tried to calm him, but he just kept yelling at them, "I know my rights." In the end they walked off and left him.'

I was horrified. I was grateful for the full and frank account from the bed next door, but it seemed Dad was very upset, and confused. By the time I left he seemed calmer, and I told him I was off to try and find out what was happening. I had the great good fortune to walk down the corridor and bump straight into the doctor who had phoned me. He told me Dad was very disorientated. They had a blood test result which said he didn't have pancreatitis, but the scan was not conclusive. They would keep an eye on Dad, and see what happened.

In fact, the next day when I visited they told me Dad was being discharged. I waited for a large bag of medication, and they assured me they didn't think Dad had pancreatitis. They were discharging him into the care of our GP, and they wanted him to come back for a check-up blood test at a later date. Dad was delighted to be going home, and just wanted to get into his own familiar bed. He was exhausted, and completely baffled by what had gone on. His memory had been shot to pieces by the stress of the whole situation, and his tinnitus, which always roared up at such times, was now back with its whistles, bangs and steam trains.

Amazingly, Dad seemed to recover well once he was home, no more pains, and he was mad keen to get out and about on his big scooter. An appointment arrived for an outpatient blood test, so the little red Zoom was packed into the 106, and off we went to the hospital. We followed signs along miles of corridors, and Dad was in fine form. We came to a sign that said 'Plaster Room'. There were two rows of chairs with patients sitting waiting, facing one another, and a corridor through the middle. We obviously had to continue on down between the rows of patients.

Unfortunately there was an empty chair at the very start of the rows. The rear wheel of Dad's scooter caught the chair, and it became hooked on to the Zoom, swinging from side to side. Dad was totally unaware of the chair, and proceeded on through the rows of people at his usual full speed ahead. Patients with broken limbs were leaping for their lives, and shouting and screaming. I was trying to catch Dad, and it was chaos, as the chair kept on swinging from side to side.

A rather large lady stepped out in Dad's path at the end of the rows of patients, and forced him to stop, but not before he had run over her foot. 'Who do you think you are?' she screamed, 'b***** Stirling Moss?' It turned out the lady was the one who took the blood, and I wouldn't have wanted to be in Dad's shoes that day.

12

The Flood

My ME seemed to be well in the background, and I was coping. I needed all my dietary supplements, but while I was careful to take them, and follow my own rules about pacing my activity, I was managing. Freddie worked hard to keep an ample supply of fizzy drinks on the supermarket shelves. He was in a routine, and that was safe for him. He never complained, and he was always ready to help at home.

There had been a few occasions when Dad had snapped at Freddie, and it had usually been a misunderstanding. Dad found it hard to open his bedroom window, and was always declaring Freddie had locked it. In the end, to keep the peace, I took charge of the key for the window lock, so I knew what was going on. It was very out of character for Dad to snap. He was once described by one of my friends as 'such a thoroughly nice guy'. He was generous to a fault, friendly, and loved life. He had a brilliant sense of humour, which got him out of many a scrape. Everyone loved Dad, and it was hard to see his character slowly changing.

He was always up for a trip away whenever John and Freddie had time off work. He hadn't seen his brother, who lived in Shropshire, for a few years. We decided it would be a good opportunity to book a week's holiday in Wales, and stop in

Shropshire on the way. It was great to see my auntie and uncle again, and to hear Dad and Uncle Bobby laughing together about their days in the Salvation Army band in Battersea. My cousin, who lived in Wales, hatched a plan to drive Auntie Edie and Uncle Bobby to our holiday bungalow, so our fathers could have more time together. We all gathered at the bungalow before taking the short walk to the little restaurant we had booked for lunch. Dad's knees, despite each one having been replaced, had become very stiff and awkward. We put it down to the fact that Dad didn't walk anywhere outside the house. His obsession with his scooters meant he refused to leave them outside any shop he wanted to enter. I knew from what he had told me about the chemist in Leighton Buzzard that he was banned from there, and I had conjured up a picture in my head of how many displays he had probably demolished. How many other places had banned him which I didn't know about?

In front of the relatives, Dad decided to show everyone how fast, and good, his scooter riding had become. Being on holiday he was riding the little Zoom. He went charging up a small step he obviously hadn't seen, tipped the scooter, and spun the wheels on gravel. We all dashed forward to catch him as he was about to hit a wall. Dad was fine, but I thought my auntie was going to have a heart attack! Our nerves in tatters, we all sat down to eat lunch, with my auntie whispering in my ear, 'I don't know how you cope!'

The weather was fine that week, and we were staying just outside the little seaside town of Aberdovey. It is a charming little place, with boats in the harbour, and a beautiful sandy beach. The houses and shops that face the beach are all painted in pastel shades. There are several little cafés with tables and chairs outside, and it is a very tranquil little spot to sit and watch the world go by. Our usual practice was to park the car, unload

Dad's scooter, and walk along the pavement with him. We were all nice and relaxed, walking past the cafés, until Dad managed to knock the leg of a chair outside a café with his scooter wheel. The poor lady sitting on the chair had just raised her coffee cup to her mouth. The coffee shot in the air, and then all down her clothes. Dad was very upset when he saw what had happened, and apologised to the lady profusely. He was so concerned, and apologetic, the lady didn't have the heart to tell him off. I apologised too, wishing the ground would open up and swallow me, and the obviously very charming lady didn't make a fuss. John and Freddie had bolted round the next corner. It was a typical day in my life at that time.

Back home, Dad was once again into his daily routine, which meant thrashing his big scooter through the fields, and along the canal towpath. I had heard from friends that he often made for our local canal-side pub, and stopped for a quick coffee, or lager, before continuing on his way. One day he made it to the town, and halfway home, when his scooter failed to go any further. He used his mobile phone to call me, and I jumped in the car to look for him. He was sitting, fortunately, at the road side, not far from home, and he certainly did not have his happy face on. I had assumed when he phoned that he had run out of charge again. It was getting very embarrassing, knocking on people's doors asking if I could buy some of their electricity, and leaving Dad's scooter on charge in their drives and garages. This time it wasn't the power, it was obviously something more serious. He was near some retirement flats, so I asked if we could leave Dad's machine until the evening, when John and Freddie could look at it.

The mobility shop van called again, and this time it was bad news. The verdict was that the Zoom Basher had finally 'killed' scooter number four. 'Thrashed to death', was the term the man

155

used! Dad was furious: the shop was no good, the mechanics were useless, and they sold rubbish. He blamed everybody and everything, and he truly, honestly, didn't think he was at fault. The manager of the shop had a quiet word with me on the phone, and suggested a really big, chunky machine might be the answer. He said he realised nothing short of a quad bike was going to be what Dad needed.

I asked what the speed range would be, and of course, it was much faster than the previous scooters. 'I can't give him anything that goes that fast,' I said. 'I might as well give him a hand grenade and be done with it.'

The manager thought for a while, and said, 'Well, we might be able to take it back to the factory in Coventry, and get them to turn the speed down on the motor. Leave it with me.'

I made it clear that Dad was not to find out about reducing the speed, or he would be furious. The van came with the new chunky model for Dad to try, with the mechanic walking beside him up and down our road. He told Dad he was on his way to deliver this particular machine to someone, but if Dad liked it, they would order him one the same. Dad was disappointed he couldn't have that one, but accepted he could wait a few days for his own to arrive. The shop made their visit to Coventry, and Dad's new 'customised' model was delivered. We made sure it came with solid tyres, as we had experience of punctures. Dad couldn't wait to try it out. He was like a kid with a new toy every time he had a new scooter. It was a good thing we had sold his house, as all his money seemed to be spent at the mobility shop. We felt that at age 90 it was his money, and he should enjoy it while he could. Scooter number five was on the road, even if this one was modified, and he didn't know it. I was just clinging on to Mum's statement that I wasn't to worry about Dad when he was out and about, as she was looking after him.

That was all very well, but my hair was turning grey at quite a speed, despite Maureen's best efforts.

It must have been a whole week before Dad came home for his lunch very annoyed. It turned out that when he was riding along the Riverside Walk, he had been overtaken by another scooter. Thank goodness he had no idea what we had done. He was very proud of the array of lights across the front of this new friend. It had suspension, and a big comfortable seat. Even if he did get overtaken, he was still pretty pleased with himself. That was, until the afternoon he came home with a large chunk of the front wing missing.

'How did you manage to do that?' I asked. It turned out he had some how pranged it into the door of the disabled toilets at Morrisons. Straight away his painting trousers came out of the wardrobe, and from the scooter basket he produced boxes of fibreglass filler, and new cans of spray paint. I had hoped to avoid the respray game for rather longer, but in no time at all we had the wrong shade of red all over the scooter, the drive, and a laundry basket I had foolishly left too close.

All patched up, he was back on the road again. It wasn't long before he came in saying he had lost another chunk of wing. He seemed really upset, saying he needed the missing piece to be able to make a good repair. He wasn't sure where it had dropped off, but he had searched and couldn't find it. I really didn't understand how a piece could just drop off, but I decided I would walk into town, and retrace his route. People must have thought I was a bit mad, searching in the gutters, but hopefully they thought I had lost an earring! When I reached Halfords, and I hadn't found any lumps of scooter wing, I suddenly realised he had probably been riding around in the shop, and could well have lost it in there. I went in, and looked around for any signs of devastation to displays, and then underneath one of the stands I found the missing piece. An assistant came up and asked if I needed help. I thought to myself that I must need help searching around the floor of Halfords: what had I become?

I went into Dad's room and said to him, 'Close your eyes, and hold out your hand.' I placed the broken red specimen in his hand. He opened his eyes, and when he saw what I had found, you would have thought he had just been given the Crown jewels.

His memory was getting to the stage where, when we were all sitting down to dinner, he would tell us the same thing over and over again. We knew he couldn't help it, and we just ignored it, but for our own sanity we started to count how many times he repeated something, and make bets on the total.

It seemed as if the rain would never stop that July, and the fields were becoming waterlogged. Dad was given strict instructions to stay out of the fields. It was about coffee time on a Saturday morning when I received a call from Dad's mobile.

He said, 'Can you come and get me? Wear your wellies, I am stuck in a flood.'

'Where are you?' I asked.

'The Riverside Walk,' he said.

I knew that was bad news as it was a long way from the road. John was busy in the garden, so I ran out to break the news to him. He threw down his gloves and shears, and said, 'That is the silliest thing he has done to date. How the hell are we going to get him home from there?' We have no idea to this day what made him think his new machine was amphibious.

Annabelle has always called me Baldrick, because she says I have a cunning plan for everything. I suggested I would ride Dad's Zoom along the road, and down the path to Dad. Freddie was at home, so if John and Freddie drove the car to the nearest point in the road, we would all wear our wellies, and see if we could push Dad's scooter to the road. Dad could ride his Zoom home, once we had got him out of the water. I set off on the Zoom, hoping I wouldn't meet too many people I knew, and was first on the scene.

Dad by this time had paddled his way out of the water, and had wringing wet socks, shoes and trousers. I sat him on his Zoom, and when John and Freddie arrived we pushed the big scooter out of the water. Fortunately it wasn't deep enough to come over our wellies. It was a long hard push for the three of us to get it up the hill to the car. Dad decided he would help by riding behind and pushing with his walking stick! Once at the car, we weren't sure how, or if, we could get this new big monster into the car. Having an estate car, we were able to flatten the back seat, but it was still a heavy object to lift. I think John and Freddie enlisted the help of some friendly passers-by, and managed to heave the scooter into the car.

John's sense of humour was fading fast. Dad was asking for the scooter to be removed from the car so that he could mend it. John said the only place the scooter was going was back to the mobility shop. The motor was underneath the footplate and had been totally immersed in the water. He was going to drive the car to the shop after lunch, and get the mechanics to help unload. He doubted very much that anyone could repair the motor.

Dad was livid and went to his room to find his scooter handbook, and paperwork. In rifling through his papers he found the swing ticket I had removed from the little charging unit, which had been in a separate box. It read 'Made in China'. John meanwhile had been to the mobility shop. They said they would have to send the motor back to the factory in Coventry, but the factory had just closed for its two-week annual summer holiday. In the meantime they would do their best to dry the motor out. John explained this to Dad, who immediately flew into a rage, saying it was all nonsense, he had found the ticket that said the scooter was made in China. He had been sold absolute rubbish from China, and now they were sending his scooter back to China for repair. He didn't fall for their nonsense about Coventry. It didn't matter how we tried to reason with him, he had made his mind up, and that was it. The following weeks were very difficult. Dad took to thrashing his Zoom into town and back each day, and we were all heartily sick of hearing about China.

I had occasion to see our GP, and I had a word with her about Dad. She felt Dad ought to have a memory test, but Dad would have to request it himself. At our next routine visit for the renewal of Dad's prescription, the GP asked Dad about his memory. She asked if he would like an appointment for a memory test, and I joked with Dad, 'Say yes if it's free', and we all laughed. Dad did say 'Yes', so the wheels were set in motion.

The drying out of the scooter motor took longer than any of us had imagined. The mobility shop felt it was best to completely dry it naturally before it went to the factory. This, of course, just added fuel to fire, as Dad saw it as more evidence his scooter had been put on a slow boat to China.

Dad's appointment for his memory test came through, and I had to take him to Houghton Regis, to the Memory Clinic. Dad was all smiles and jokes with the lady who took him to do the test, and when it was finished he came out just as happy. 'She said well done to me,' he said. He took this simple remark to heart, and the more it was repeated, the better his efforts had become. By the time John was told about the test, the lady had said he had done 'extremely well'!

Sue, hearing tales on the phone from Dad about his rubbish

scooter that had been sent to China, asked if we would like to take Dad down to stay with her for a couple of weeks. She could tell we were in need of another break, and we took her up on the offer. While Dad was away, the mobility shop phoned to say they had sent Dad's motor to the factory. The factory had looked at it and declared it useless. As the scooter was still under guarantee they were replacing it with a new motor. This was amazing news, but I reminded the shop that the old one had been modified for speed. They agreed to organise that, and let us know when the scooter was all done and dusted, or in Dad's case scrubbed clean.

We picked Dad up from Sue's and his first question was, 'Have they sent my scooter back from China yet?' The mobility shop van arrived, and after two months of being parted from his beloved machine, Dad and the scooter were reunited. He was out and about terrorising the town once more. The end of the narrow boat season on the canal was approaching. I tried explaining to Dad that it was a really bad idea riding along the towpath. In summer, if he broke down, we had the possibility of getting his scooter on to a boat to get it to a road, but in winter we would be very stuck. Probably to keep me quiet, he agreed, but I knew it was getting harder to reason with him as whatever I said he would probably forget in five minutes.

One Sunday morning the day started bright and sunny, and Dad was on his scooter and away before we could finish washing up the breakfast dishes. It wasn't long before the rain clouds gathered, and the rain started to fall in buckets. We knew Dad had a big rain cape in his scooter basket, which covered him and the whole machine. We didn't know where he was, but it was no use phoning him as he didn't hear his phone. We just had to hope he was in a coffee shop somewhere.

At midday a large van drew up outside. Dad got out of the

passenger seat, and a gentleman came to the door. He had seen Dad soaked to the skin in the Country Park, which is in a village just outside Leighton Buzzard. He was worried about Dad riding home in such conditions, and with his son's help had put Dad's scooter in his van. We were very grateful for this man's kindness, thanked him profusely, and gave him a bottle of wine for taking the trouble to bring Dad home. We felt very embarrassed, as it made us look so uncaring. He probably thought we had turned Dad out of the house on a terrible day, just to get him out of our hair.

We told Dad it wasn't a good idea to be riding so far. He was not only caught out in the rain, but he could have run out of charge going such a distance. It was too dangerous riding on roads without pavements. We knew we were wasting our breath, because he wouldn't remember, but it had to be said. No appointment was forthcoming to get the results of Dad's memory test; we had been told we would need to see the doctor in charge of the unit for that, and there would be a wait. An appointment did come through for the Elderly Persons Unit, but it was just the routine visit that was part of my backup.

The day we left in the car for Houghton Regis, Dad was in a bad frame of mind. He was very agitated about the appointment. I tried to reassure him that it was only a routine visit, just like the previous ones, and there was no need to worry about it. 'I can't think why I am doing this,' he complained in the car. 'This guy will think I am stupid going to see him again. It is embarrassing for him, and me, he knows there is nothing wrong with me.'

When we were called into the consulting room, Dad went in with all guns blazing. Before he even sat down he started telling the doctor how active he was. All about his scooter, and how he rode to the Country Park and back. How silly I was telling him the police would tell him off for riding in the road. A police car came along and waved to him. He was a really good rider, and he found it so enjoyable being able to be out and about in the countryside. I couldn't believe my ears, and the doctor was looking at him a bit puzzled. Finally, the doctor asked where the Country Park was. What kind of road was it that it didn't have pavements? Was it a flat straight road, and how much traffic used it?

'Well, it's a bit hilly around the entrance to the sandpit,' Dad said.

'What traffic uses the sandpit?' the doctor asked.

'Oh, a few lorries,' said Dad.

'Now let's get this straight. You ride your mobility scooter along a B class road, with no pavements, it is used by the sand pit lorries, and there is a bit of a dip in the road. So when you are the other side of the dip a sand lorry could come along and plough straight into you. It doesn't have to be a sand lorry, any traffic could come along, you are going at a much slower speed. You could kill yourself, and cause a terrible accident.'

I thought, 'Oh Dad, what have you done now.'

The doctor turned to me and said, 'I am afraid I will have to contact the DVLA for advice. When I am told something like this it is my duty to tell the DVLA. I am bound by law, and I don't have a choice.' Still looking at me he said, 'You will have to see he doesn't ride along this road.'

I thought, 'This man cannot be serious', and said, 'Dad's memory is such that five minutes after I tell him something he has forgotten. I can't stop him.'

The doctor pulled a sheet of paper from his desk and started to write. It was a letter addressed to Dad. It set out the fact that he was not to ride on any B class roads without pavements until the DVLA had given a ruling on the situation. He told me that

163

if Dad did ride on B class roads, I was to take his scooter keys away. Two copies of the letter were made, and we were both told to sign.

This was a nightmare as far as I was concerned. It was not the routine chat I was expecting, and what a fine mess Dad had now landed both of us in. We came away with the doctor saying he would let us know what the DVLA advised. Dad was all boastful still, and said to me, 'Silly fool, I shall ride where I want', and I could see trouble ahead. It was in fact a couple of weeks before the doctor phoned to say the DVLA had told him the rules on mobility scooters were not clear cut, but while they looked into it, Dad wasn't allowed on B class roads. I pleaded for him to be allowed to continue riding into town along the pavements, and this was agreed.

I told Dad what had been said, and that this was serious. He had been bragging to the doctor, and this was the outcome. He was not to ride to the Country Park any more, and if I found out he had, I would have no choice but to take his keys away. Dad was unrepentant and I just knew things could get nasty.

13

Alzheimer's

John reached the age of 65. He retired from work, and we had a party to celebrate. It was a whole new routine for the household with John at home, but of course Freddie was still working. We joked with him about being the only breadwinner in the house, and how he was now looking after a pack of oldies.

Dad was still out and about, and I was always reminding him 'pavements only'. I happened to be in town, and bumped into an old friend. She told me she thought I ought to know that Dad was riding past her house on the pavement, but on bin days, when all the bins were put out, Dad was swerving round the bins straight out onto the main road and back, without looking.

I returned home very worried, and then as I was putting the lunch on the table Dad burst in through the door. With a big grin on his face he said, 'I have just been to the Country Park, it was lovely there this morning.'

I was furious. I said, 'Dad you know you are not allowed to ride along that road, you have been banned.'

'Oh, I am not taking any notice of that silly old fool,' Dad said.

My heart was pounding, and I knew I had to take action. I said, 'I am really sorry you told me that, because now I shall have to take your scooter keys away. I have had to sign to say you won't ride on that road, and I am responsible for you.'

'Nonsense,' said Dad, and sat down to eat his lunch.

When we were on our own, I discussed the situation with John. 'I have to take his keys away,' I said.

John said, 'Well if you do, he is going to get very annoyed.'

The next day Dad went to the cupboard to get his keys. I called to him, 'Dad, I told you yesterday, I have had to take your keys away.'

He became angrier than I had ever seen him, he went red and purple in the face, strode across the kitchen, and slammed the door behind him. He then slammed the outer door, and went off walking to the main road with the aid of his two sticks. By lunch time he hadn't returned, so by three o'clock I phoned the library, and various places I thought he frequented.

Nobody had seen him. By the time Freddie had finished work at six o'clock he still hadn't appeared, so John and Freddie went out in the car looking for him. They found him walking along the road near home, and stopped, and he climbed into the car. He was still angry when he came into the kitchen. 'I don't want any dinner,' he said, as he waved a bag of fruit at me, and made his way to his sitting room.

The three of us sat down to dinner, and after we had eaten I plucked up my courage to take him a cup of tea.

'I want the phone,' he said, 'I want to speak to Sue, I don't want to live here any more, I want to live with Sue.'

I went to get the phone for him and said to John, 'He wants to live with Sue.'

'That's the best news I have heard today,' he joked.

After Dad's call I phoned Sue and we had a long chat. She said the best thing to do was take him down to her. She would sort his room out the next day, and then if we could drive him down the following day, which would be a Saturday, we could all stay overnight. Dad slammed out again the next day, and while he was out I set to work packing a case for him.

When he came in he was all smiles, walked into his room, and said, 'What is this case doing here?'

'We are taking you to Sue's tomorrow,' I said. 'You phoned Sue yesterday, and asked her if you could live with her.'

'Don't be silly,' he said. 'I did no such thing.'

I picked up the phone and put it in his hand. 'Phone Sue and ask her,' I said.

He couldn't believe what we were telling him, he had no recollection of the call at all. Sue said we were to continue with our plan, and we were to have a break.

We returned from Lymington on the Sunday, and by Monday Sue was on the phone. 'Dad is just sobbing,' she said. 'He says he doesn't want to be here, he wants to be in Leighton Buzzard.' We agreed to pick him up and bring him back the following weekend.

Within days of being back we had more bad temper, and tantrums about the lack of scooter riding. He said he badly wanted to go to the Country Park and have a cup of tea, so I took him in the car. That didn't suit, so he said he wanted to go to the library. I organised the local Buzzer Bus to pick him up, drop him off, and collect him two hours later. When the Buzzer Bus arrived, a wonderfully patient lady came to collect him, and he asked her to take him to the canal and push him in!

I was phoning the Memory Clinic in Houghton Regis, asking how much longer we would have to wait for our appointment. We needed to see the doctor urgently, to get the results of Dad's memory test. It appeared they were in the middle of changing their system, and moving the Memory Clinic to different premises. We just had to wait. I went to see the GP, hoping she could give us something to calm Dad. After his antics at the Barton unit I was concerned he would get suicidal again. She said I was the third one she had seen that day, asking for help for an elderly person in their care. She added, looking at me, 'The others were in tears.' It seemed we just had to wait for the Houghton Regis appointment. And what if Dad refused to go?

I was beginning to feel exhausted, and on the edge of a real ME breakdown again. John said he had worked hard all his life to enjoy his retirement, and this was not what he wanted. Sue was worried about all of us. Dad's latest stunt was to ask for his Power of Attorney so he could tear it up. When we said we didn't have it, he went on a tour of the solicitors in the town to see if he could find it. He found the right office, who gave him an appointment for the following week. Things were getting difficult, so we literally ran him out of town and took him to Sue's.

Again we had big discussions with Sue, and we both agreed things had to change. Dad had become verbally aggressive towards me, and confrontational about everything. He just wasn't the same person, he wasn't my Dad any more. To cope, I was now thinking of him as 'Mr Dementia'. Sue suggested she should do a tour of the residential care homes in Lymington, to see what she could find out. I hated the thought of Dad having to go into a home, I felt I had failed, and I felt guilty. Sue also said we couldn't keep driving the 125 miles to Lymington and back, so she would meet us halfway. We found a car park, with toilets, in Hungerford, and that became our meeting point. We would take boxes of sandwiches, sit in the car, eat lunch, and then exchange Dad.

Sue's research of the homes revealed that Dad would have to agree that he wanted to live there. Also, we would have to have a diagnosis of Dad's illness. The fees were exceedingly high, but at the age of 92 we figured we had to spend his money on the best home for him. The other minor point was that they were all full, so it was a case of going on the waiting list. Sue put his name down for the one she thought most appropriate, and we would have to think how we were going to sort out the other problems later.

We had waited a total of six months before we received an appointment to see the doctor at the Memory Clinic in Houghton Regis. Getting Dad there was going to be a major problem, but we had to try. Life at home was pretty intolerable for all of us. Freddie was getting shouted at for things he could not help, and it hurt me that Freddie was taking stick. John and I could reason it out that this wasn't Dad, and none of it was meant, but Freddie couldn't. We had even taken to hiding the knives at night in case Dad got hold of them. The appointment date was approaching. Sue spent time on the phone trying to convince Dad he must attend. He told her he had no intention of going anywhere near the silly old fool he had seen there before.

It was our routine at that time for the care agency ladies to come in and bath Dad two mornings a week. It so happened that the appointment date fell on a bathing day. It was an afternoon appointment, so it didn't matter. As the ladies arrived I had a quick word with them about the situation. I then took Freddie to work. As I returned they were leaving.

They said, 'You won't have any trouble. We have wound him up, saying he must go and stand up for himself. He must have his say. He is gunning for them in Houghton Regis now.' Laughing, they fled, and I was still not sure it would be that easy. I told myself Mum must be on the case, and she would see we had the right outcome.

Later that day Dad quietly put his hat and coat on, and

presented himself in the kitchen in good time for our drive to Houghton Regis. Nothing was said, we just threw on our coats, and left before Dad changed his mind. An extremely nice gentleman called us all in for our appointment, and it was obvious that he was the Big White Chief. He reminded Dad about the test he had taken, and said his diagnosis was a mixture of dementia and Alzheimer's. He gave us the statistics for the number of people who suffer from the mixture, and told us about all the various kinds of Alzheimer's.

Dad had been listening carefully, and at the sound of the word 'dementia' he banged his fist on the table, and shouted at the doctor, 'I did very well in that memory test.' It was clear the doctor had seen and heard it all before. He was calm and polite to Dad. He said, 'I have the written report here of the test, if you wish to contest it, I am sure we can make arrangements for you to talk to the lady who carried out the test.' Dad just became more and more annoyed, and I felt very embarrassed.

An assistant came into the room and spoke to Dad, and guided him to the door. The doctor stood up, and whilst Dad's attention was taken, he had a quiet word with us. He suggested we contact the Alzheimer's Society for information. He said he didn't think the Alzheimer's drug was appropriate in Dad's case. He could see we were having a hard time coping, and pointed out he couldn't make recommendations, but if we looked on the internet, we would find ratings for the various care homes. I think we were all shell-shocked as we trooped out to the car, Dad shuffling along with his two sticks, and red in the face with anger.

Sue was waiting anxiously for a phone call, and as soon as I had made everyone a cup of tea I disappeared out of earshot, and phoned her. 'We continue with our plans for your holiday,' she said, 'It is only another week until you come to the Isle of Wight. Dad will come to me, and I will have to try to persuade him he would be better off in a really good care home. He knows his friend Geoff was in a very nice home, and I will tell him it would be nice for him to be near me.' I liked Sue's optimism, but I didn't share it.

The following week I started packing and looking forward to our trip to the Isle of Wight. The day we left, the suitcases, and Dad's Zoom, were all loaded, and we piled into the car. As we drew out of the drive Dad looked back at the house and waved it goodbye!

Once on the island we all sighed with relief, and just lapped up the peace, and the ability to relax. I love the seaside, and I also have fond memories of beach huts from my childhood. We were exploring along a cliff path when I decided to be nosey. I wanted to see the view from the beach huts. Not looking where I was going, I turned and caught my foot in a rabbit hole. I fell straight to the ground. John and Freddie came running to pick me up, but I knew from the feel of my foot I had either sprained, or torn, a ligament. I couldn't put any weight on my foot, and I could feel it swelling. I hobbled to the sea with the help of John and Freddie, and stood with my feet in the cold water. We were in a place where John could park the car nearby, so he fetched the car and drove us back to base. I had two sports injury ice packs, which I always keep in the freezer, even on holiday, so I sat with my feet up for the rest of the day. John and Freddie were despatched to the Red Cross shop in Freshwater, and came back with a pair of crutches.

I was still hopping around on my crutches a couple of days later when I received a phone call from Sue. The preferred care home had phoned to say if Dad wanted it, they would have a vacancy the following Tuesday. She thought she would take Dad to have a look round, and meet the matron. It so happened that our return ferry was on that Tuesday, so we could go

171

straight to her house and help her, if Dad agreed to it. 'If Dad agreed to it' were the operative words: neither of us could see it being straightforward.

Over the next few days I had phone calls from Sue with updates. Dad had been all smiles with the matron, and they had talked about Geoff, and how they had been friends for so many years. He had admired all that he had seen, and was like Dad again. When they arrived home, he suddenly became Mr Dementia once more.

On the Saturday, it was a beautiful sunny day. Blue skies, and just a light breeze, one of those days when it is heavenly being at the seaside. We received a call from our good friends Janice and Bryan saying, 'It's a beautiful day, how about us coming over on the ferry, and joining you for the day?' We loved their visits, it was like the old days again when we had spent holidays together. Lots of fun and laughter, just what we needed. I prepared some salad for lunch, and gave John and Freddie a list of good things they could get in the deli in Yarmouth, while I sat on a seat and watched for the ferry to approach.

As I sat there, my phone rang, and it was Sue. 'I am having awful trouble with Dad, he is now saying he is refusing to go into the care home. Can you come and speak to him? One of the boys will pick you up at the ferry terminal.'

Janice and Bryan were just coming in on the ferry, and I was getting onto my feet with the aid of my crutches. At the sight of my crutches there were cries of 'What have you done?'

'Oh, I have only fallen down a rabbit hole,' I said, and there were laughs all round.

It was a good thing they were such good friends. I was able to say, 'We are heading back for lunch, then can you take Freddie to the swimming pool, while John and I catch the ferry to Lymington. We have to go and sort out trouble with Dad.'

It was a very long hop on my crutches, on and off the ferry, but we were at Sue's in 45 minutes. By the time we arrived, Dad had calmed down, and I think Sue had weathered most of the storm without us. It was so difficult talking, and trying to reason, with someone who forgets the first half of your sentence before you get to the end. We returned to the Isle of Wight, and spent the rest of the day with Janice and Bryan, who declared they had enjoyed their afternoon with Freddie.

My foot was gradually getting better, and on the Monday we returned my crutches to the Red Cross shop with thanks. Those crutches, together with the on-site luggage trolley, had been invaluable. John and Freddie had become used to pushing me on the trolley, back and forth between the bungalow and the car, and numerous people had stopped to ask what I had done. It was always met with laughter when I confessed that, in the process of being nosey, I had fallen down a rabbit hole.

We packed our belongings and left the holiday bungalow early on the Tuesday. We all knew there was trouble ahead. Only the day before, Sue had passed the phone to Dad so that he could talk to me. I had to talk tough, and I hated it. I had to tell him we were not taking him back to Leighton Buzzard. He needed medical help which we couldn't give, and he couldn't stay at Sue's, as she had a business to run. He was going to be fine in the home. Geoff had been very happy there. Dad was adamant he was not going into any home.

It seemed exceedingly quiet when we entered Sue's house. Dad was dressed, sitting in a chair, and looking dejected. Sue and her eldest son helped Dad into Sue's car, and all Dad's luggage was in the boot. We drove to the home, and with Dad in a wheelchair, we walked in silence into the reception area. The staff were jolly and bright, and helped Dad into the lift. Sue and I went up to Dad's room, while the menfolk carried the luggage. The staff arrived with cups of tea, and we were all saying, 'What a lovely room.' Dad insisted on opening a window, and then saw building works. There was a new kitchen extension being added, and Dad immediately declared it was going to be far too noisy. We told him that if it was, he could shut the window, but he wasn't in a positive mood, and nothing was going to suit.

Sue did a runner, to help with the remainder of the luggage, while I unpacked Dad's clothes and put them on hangers in the wardrobe. Dad started to cry. He wouldn't look at me, or speak to me. I felt dreadful, but I just had to tell myself this wasn't Dad, it was Mr Dementia. It didn't help much, but it was probably one of the hardest things I have ever had to do. Sue returned and whispered to me to go. I joined John and Freddie, and we all drove back to Leighton Buzzard wondering how this was all going to turn out.

How Sue coped in those early days I am not sure. Dad had decided both Sue and I were a couple of wicked witches. He moaned endlessly to Sue about the noise driving him mad. He said the building work was unrelenting, they worked all through the night, and it had made his tinnitus unbearable. When Sue asked the matron about the building work, she said, 'Oh, they are on holiday at the moment, there is nothing going on.' Within a few weeks another room became available, so to placate Dad he was moved across the corridor. That didn't suit of course, and Sue was still in trouble. The Elderly Persons Unit at Barton took Dad back on their books, and visited him. They immediately arranged for Dad to be put on the Alzheimer's drug. Friends were visiting him, and the staff were saying what a nice guy Dad was. How bright and cheerful. Sue gradually became aware that as wicked witches she and I were the only ones being punished. He was raising his game for everyone else.

Matron suggested that Dad could have his scooter back if he wanted. There were other residents with different kinds of mobility aids, and the home had a good covered area with charging points. There were pavements straight into town, and she felt it might help Dad. Sue phoned and said her eldest son had volunteered to drive up to Leighton Buzzard in a Land Rover. He would bring a friend so that they could collect Dad's beloved big scooter. She felt it was safer than letting him have the Zoom.

I felt Sue had no idea what she was letting herself in for, but it would certainly make Dad's eyes light up. We all discussed the situation, and decided Lymington was far better placed for pavement access to the areas Dad would want to visit. It was also quieter, with less lorry traffic. Leighton Buzzard is known as the lorry capital of the country; because of its geographical location, at that time it had more haulage companies than any other town. Once again I had a quiet word with Mum, and said, 'I hope you are serious when you say you look after Dad when he is out.'

It wasn't long before Sue was on the phone asking for the telephone number of the mobility shop. There had been more scooter breakdowns, and she needed some information to give to the local mobility shop. The repair man in Lymington couldn't stop laughing when Sue explained about the factory applying speed limitation to the motor. There was a lot going on in the home in the way of activities, trips out in the minibus, musical entertainment and fancy hat competitions. We felt we couldn't have found a better home for Dad, and he was receiving medication that was unavailable in Bedfordshire.

Back in Leighton Buzzard the house seemed very quiet. Dad had lived with us for the past five years and eight months. In that time John had retired, and Poppy had died. We all had to adjust to being on our own again. I was getting some very nasty pains in my chest, and they were shooting up through my jaw to my ear. I felt it was time I made a visit to the GP. She sent me for an immediate ECG test as she was concerned about my heart. Quite quickly I was given an appointment for the relevant clinic at Stoke Mandeville hospital. They put me on a treadmill whilst being wired to a monitor. Suffering with ME, that was difficult for me. The outcome was that I was put on a waiting list for an angiogram at a hospital in High Wycombe.

The day I had the angiogram was a mini nightmare. I wasn't allowed food or drink from early morning, and with ME and a blood sugar problem, that in itself was difficult. I was sat in a cold corner of a waiting area. There were beds there, but they were obviously for very poorly patients. I was left sitting in that chair, shivering, for hours. It wasn't anyone's fault I was left there so long. An emergency had come in, and the equipment had to be used for the poor patient having a heart attack. The system meant all the patients in the waiting area had backed up, and more and more kept coming. Some of the people waiting started to shout at the nurses, and some threatened to get dressed and leave. It made for a horrible atmosphere, and my turn for the procedure didn't come until five o'clock in the afternoon. By that time I was so weak I couldn't walk to the treatment area, and the nurse was very annoyed at having to take me in a wheelchair.

When the doctor did the angiogram, he told me it was clear. That was good news. I was given an appointment for a further consultation, and I was sent back to my cold corner. The nurse gave me a rather dirty-looking plastic jug of water, and an equally scruffy-looking plastic glass. I was told, 'You can't go until you have drunk all the water.' I dutifully drank it, as I just wanted to go and get warm.

The following week at home I began to feel worse every day. My throat started to hurt, and my glands felt tender. When I finally saw the doctor for the official result of the angiogram he couldn't understand why my throat felt bad. He said it didn't look red or sore. His diagnosis was a bit of a shock. He felt I had a nasty virus that attacks the heart, and gives chest pain, the sort of pain I was experiencing at the top of my arms. Its name was Born Holmes Disease, a form of the Coxsackie B virus. There was no treatment, and he suggested I took up to eight paracetamol a day.

It had been April when the pains first started, and it was June when Dad went into the home. I had just put everything down to ME, and stress. By December I was feeling very ill. I happened to be getting my dietary supplements in the health food shop, and the lady mentioned to me that she knew someone who had some good computer software that might confirm my diagnosis. Why didn't I try it? I had nothing else to try, so I contacted the lady. What came up on the computer screen was confirmation that I had the Coxsackie B virus, and then another virus came up which was a later one. It was Epstein-Barr, which is glandular fever.

It really answered all the questions as to why I had been feeling so bad, but where had I picked up the glandular fever? The symptoms started just after my visit to the hospital, and I hadn't been anywhere else. I had felt too ill. It was a mystery. I thought glandular fever, nicknamed the 'kissing disease', was an illness that affected young people. The only thing we could think of was the drinking water glass at the hospital, but we have no proof of that, and will never know.

Christmas was very quiet. I was feeling bad, and Dad was in the home. We decided that as it was a rare occasion for Freddie to have four consecutive days off work over Christmas, we would get up early on Boxing Day, and drive down to Lymington to have lunch at the home with Dad. Sue had been with Dad at the home all day Christmas Day, and we didn't want him to feel he didn't have visitors. When we arrived we saw a table in the little library room all set for four people, with pretty serviettes and Christmas crackers.

We met Dad in the corridor, who greeted us with his usual scowl. 'What are you doing here?' he asked.

'We have come to have lunch with you,' we said.

'Well, I am eating in the dining room,' he replied. Then pointing at the library he added, 'You eat in there.'

I had to say, 'We haven't come 125 miles to eat lunch in a room on our own, we have come to see you.'

He begrudgingly sat with us, and the whole exercise was a disaster. As soon as he had eaten, he said he was tired and going to have a sleep. We got the message that we were still being punished. On our way out we took a look at his scooter. It was looking very dented and much the worse for wear. One of the arm rests had been broken off completely.

We didn't visit very much after that, as our visits only upset him, and Sue could do without any extra trouble. There were occasions in the following year when Sue would make one of her very regular visits, and he would fly into a terrible rage. She learnt to assess his mood. If he was amenable she would take him out in the car to a tea shop, or a garden centre, but if he was looking for trouble she would leave straight away. Dad's sense of time was deserting him, so he didn't really know how long anyone had been there.

I struggled with my health all that year. I didn't take the high doses of paracetamol as I didn't want to damage my liver. I increased my supplements, and tried to rest, and rebuild my immune system. In the summer we decided to take a week's holiday on the Isle of Wight again. These breaks were tried and tested for me; we could spend time with Sue, and visit Dad.

Our visit to Dad was just as disastrous. We all sat round trying to think of things to say that wouldn't upset him, or cause an argument. We always hoped for some sort of improvement in the relationship, perhaps we had been punished enough, but we still remained in his bad books. At that particular visit I think John left the room for a short while, and Mr Dementia took the opportunity to round on me and tell me he wished he had never had me.

Sue soldiered on with her support of Dad. He was 93 by this time, and Matron had called the doctor to him a few times. His heart was getting weaker, but he was still able to drag himself out to his beloved scooter, and ride into town come what may. We were both very glad he had the medical support of the home.

Winter came and went, and by the spring I was at last feeling much stronger. A notice fell through our letter box advertising a new line-dancing class. I felt it was time I had some fun. I thought I would give it a go, and if it made me too exhausted I would have to stop. My attitude to ME has always been to push the boundaries to see where they are. I loved the music, and although I found it tiring at first, I began to strengthen my muscles. I made new friends, and I really looked forward to Thursday mornings.

Sue was in constant touch on the phone, and there were more reports of scooter troubles. Dad had received visits from the doctor again, who was now warning that Dad's heart was very weak. Matron reported to Sue that it was difficult trying to keep Dad in. There were days when they told him he wasn't well enough to go out, but of course he forgot what they had said,

179

and headed for his scooter. Matron requested that Sue take the scooter away.

As Dad was complaining the scooter wasn't working properly, she took the opportunity to get her son to pick it up and take it back to her house. Dad was told it had gone for a service and repair. When it didn't return very quickly, Dad started to get angry. At that time one of his friends in the home had just bought himself a big, shiny, all-singing, all-dancing scooter, very powerful, with lots of lights and extras. He rode it a few times, and didn't get on with it. Dad asked the friend if he could borrow it, and the friend agreed. It was a good thing the plan reached the ears of Matron, who called the friend into her office and explained he couldn't loan his scooter to Dad. The friend returned to the dining room, and told Dad he was sorry, but he couldn't borrow the scooter as Matron had said there were insurance issues.

By all accounts Dad went wild, shouting and carrying on at his friend, and scaring the ladies in the home with his outburst. Sue was told by Matron that if Dad was going to upset the other residents we would have to remove him. This shook both of us, and we began to worry what we would do if he was expelled from such a lovely home.

14

Moving On

Dad's health began to deteriorate, and Matron told Sue his heart was so weak we could lose him at any time. Sue had a chat to her friend the medium, and she told Sue that before Dad passed into the Spirit World he would see Mum. Sue reported this to me on the phone, and we did see the funny side. We could just visualise panic setting in with both of us, the minute he mentioned Mum's name.

It was a Sunday evening when the phone rang, and it was Dad. He was obviously feeling tearful, and all he kept saying was, 'Wendy, I am so sorry.' I told him he didn't have to say sorry, we understood the situation. It was a short call, and when he had finished saying sorry he put the phone down.

The next day I received a call from Sue, saying Dad's breathing was bad, so Matron had called the doctor. The doctor said he was admitting Dad to hospital. Matron had phoned Sue there and then, and Sue was able to go in the ambulance with Dad. As they entered Lymington Hospital, Dad turned to Sue and said, 'Well, is this it, then?' Sue had given reassurance, and Dad was soon installed in a bed.

Sue visited the following day, and I waited anxiously for her call. When she phoned she said, 'I have had the funniest afternoon. You will not believe it when I tell you what Dad has been saying. I don't know what they have given him, but he is as bright as a button, and chuckling away. He doesn't realise he is in hospital. He thinks he is back in his office in the days when he was a company secretary. He thinks the people in the beds opposite are all members of staff. He told me, one lady was in Accounts, and another chap was in Despatch. He said, "They don't get on of course", and continued on relating all the office gossip.' She said, 'He laughed and laughed, and I just couldn't help laughing with him. He said the Managing Director was in his office round the corner, and when the nurse came he asked her what department she was in, and whether she was happy there. Then he said, "Where have they gone?" and started looking around. "Who?" I asked. "Your mother and Geoff, they were both there a minute ago."'

I gasped, and felt a chill run down my spine when she told me. 'Oh no, he has seen Mum,' I said.

'I know,' she said, 'I couldn't wait to tell you. He is so good, though, it is just as if the old Dad is back.'

I didn't know what to make of it all. Sue was going back to see him in the evening, and promised to keep me posted.

The next morning at seven o'clock the phone beside the bed rang. I snatched it up, and it was Sue. 'Wendy,' she said, 'Dad died at four o'clock this morning.'

I was shocked. She went on to tell me he had been fine when she left him in the evening, still happy. Then the hospital phoned her just before four o'clock, saying, 'Come quickly.' She raced to the hospital, and there was someone waiting in the car park to hurry her down the corridor. As they approached the ward the Sister came running out saying, 'I am so sorry, my dear, your Dad has just gone.' It turned out he had started shouting, so they gave him something to quieten him, and his heart just became slower and slower and stopped.

We knew Dad was 94, we knew his heart was weak, but no matter how you prepare yourself the finality of the situation is hard to absorb. I did what I always do in a crisis, I started organising. We were due to take Freddie for his annual holiday in the Yorkshire Dales two days later. We had a B&B booked, and the suitcases were out for packing. John, Freddie and I had a quick conference. Freddie said he was happy to go to Yorkshire on the train. We would cancel our arrangements, and once we had put Freddie on the train at Milton Keynes, we would go down to Lymington to stay with Sue. We phoned my cousin, and her husband the Methodist minister, and imparted the news. While Freddie was away, Sue, John and I worked hard organising a funeral.

It was good to be with Sue, we had both been through a lot in the 12 years and 8 months since Mum died. We talked about how lucky we were that we had our proof of life after death. Sue and I were able to talk about how happy Mum and Dad and all the family would be, back together again. We laughed and said Dad would be playing his brass band music already. We also cried, as we had lost both parents now. Human beings are made of emotions, and it doesn't matter how much proof you have that your loved ones live on, you still feel loss.

Freddie's supermarket were very understanding about our circumstances, and said Freddie could take his three days' bereavement leave straight after his holiday. That meant we were able to pick Freddie up from his holiday, and have the weekend at home, before we all returned to Lymington for the funeral.

Sue had a glut of tomatoes from her greenhouse, so I came back with a huge quantity, and proceeded to make gallons of tomato soup. The day of the funeral was quite cool and cloudy for July, but just warm enough to set up a table and plenty of

183

chairs in Sue's garden. I was in charge of the soup kitchen, and as all the relatives congregated at Sue's house before the funeral cars arrived, we all sat out in the garden with hot soup and bread rolls. The church near 'Franfay', where we held Mum's funeral, was busy with a children's school holiday club, so David, our family minister, was able to get permission to use the church in the High Street. It was the church where John and I had married, and our friends Janice and Bryan, and it was also where I had been the vicar's confirmation candidate from hell!

When the funeral cars arrived at Sue's house, we all piled in. We were just a few streets away from the church when our driver said, 'Ladies and gentlemen, we have a problem', and pulled the car into the side of the road. We realised the engine had cut out. The hearse in front also stopped, and one of the funeral directors walked back to have a word with our driver. Sue and I exchanged glances. We knew what the other was thinking: 'This is Dad, he is having a joke with us to the end.' We tried not to laugh, because it didn't seem fitting in a funeral car, but we were stifling the giggles. The driver apologised profusely, saying he would just let the engine cool for a few minutes, and then when he started it we were away and going again.

We passed the building where Dad had worked as company secretary, and we drove up the steep hill that is Lymington High Street, past the bank he had opened in 1952. It all seemed very appropriate. Our cousin and her husband were waiting to greet us at the church, just as they had done for Mum's funeral. It was so good to be surrounded by family. As we followed the coffin into church with its covering of white lilies, I caught sight of Dad's elderly next-door neighbour looking very bereft. I stepped out of the line of mourners to squeeze her hand for a second. I know what made me do it: it was what Dad would

184

have done. On a dull day the sun shone on the coffin, just as it had at Mum's funeral, and we all followed it out of the church to the cemetery.

As we stood beside the grave, at just the same spot where I had stood beside Dad at Mum's funeral, I remembered what I had whispered in Dad's ear, 'It's not Mum in that box', and I was able to think, 'And it is not Dad in this box either.'

'Franfay' having been sold, we made our way from the cemetery to Dad's favourite restaurant, in a hotel in the village of Sway. Dad had a large collection of beautiful photographs he had taken, all enlarged and printed in the bathroom at 'Franfay', of course. There were so many that we didn't know what to do with them, so we stood them all around the room at the restaurant, and asked everyone to choose one to take away in memory of Dad.

The next day we left Sue's house, and returned to Leighton Buzzard. It was the end of another chapter in our lives, and we now had to move on. Sue had to dispose of Dad's possessions, and John and I had to deal with the paperwork. Sue and I had worked as a team looking after Mum and Dad in their later years, and we continued to make decisions about everything together.

Christmas brought lots of memories, as Christmas always does, and it was a quiet one for us. On Christmas Day I had used the musical cake slice to cut the Christmas pudding. Traditions in families continue, even the little things like the cake slice that plays 'Jingle Bells'! It always made Dad laugh. After the washing up was done, and we had all settled in the lounge, the strains of 'Happy Birthday' came from the kitchen. There was nobody in the kitchen. The button on the cake slice had to be pressed to make it play. I looked at Freddie, and he looked at me, and we walked out to the kitchen to see what was happening. The cake slice was playing away all on its own, where I had left it, on the work surface. I just laughed and said 'Happy Christmas, Dad'.

It was Mothering Sunday on 4th April 2011. Dad had always come home on his scooter just before Mothering Sunday with either flowers for me, or more usually a huge plant. It didn't happen towards the end when he was Mr Dementia. I decided I would go to the Spiritualist meeting that night.

As the meeting progressed, one of the mediums started to hand out red roses to everyone who received a message. He said he didn't know why he had been told to do it, he was just doing as he was told by Spirit. The last message that evening was mine. Calling out Dad's name he said, 'Can anyone take this name?' I put my hand up. I knew the message was meant for me, because not only was it Dad's name, Dad had always maintained mediums should give names. Dad had managed to give me a flower even though he wasn't on Earth.

I decided that if Dad was now able to give a red rose on Mothering Sunday, he was obviously in a fit state to communicate through a medium. I know it can take time for people to recover when they go to the next world, especially if they have been very ill. As it was my next-door neighbour's birthday, I suggested to her that we should each have a private reading with a medium. I would book them, and her reading would be her birthday present from me. I keep an exercise book in which I write all my messages through mediums, while they are fresh in my mind. My book tells me it was the 13th April 2011 when I received the following message.

The medium said, 'I have a gentleman here who couldn't get you in the room fast enough. What he is saying is "Apologies needed". He is talking about all the pain from arthritis. His problems started at the age of 72. He also had tummy problems.

186

I feel he had wonderful manners. His manners meant he was always well dressed in his early years, a shirt and tie, a suit, and clean shoes, but in the later years he wore jumpers. Jeans would always have been a no no.' This was all very correct. Then Dad went on to talk about his memory problems.

There was a lot of talk about the paperwork we were doing for him at that time, then the medium said, 'He is telling me you are very worried about how things should be sorted out for your son's future. He says look at his strengths, not his weaknesses. Look back at what he has achieved, and talk to him about what he wants. He says you will be told you can't have the funding you want, and you will just accept it, when others would not. You are straight down the line with it, but don't be afraid to do your own thing.' I came home on a high, feeling I knew for sure Dad was back as himself again, not Mr Dementia any more.

John and I had been realising, as we sorted out Dad's will, that we needed to make wills ourselves, and think about the future for Freddie. All parents with an adult son or daughter who has a learning disability worry. We didn't honestly know where to begin. We knew the Council had some flats for people with learning disabilities, but we also knew there weren't any vacancies, and that they were like gold dust to get. Freddie was now 32, living happily at home with us, working in the supermarket, and very settled. We were happy with the situation, but we knew we had to make arrangements for our old age, and eventual death. We decided we should phone Social Services and ask for Freddie to be assessed. A friend had told us this was our first step. So I took a deep breath and made the call.

A couple of weeks later a gentleman from the Adult Learning Disability Team came to see us, and Freddie. He told us about a carers group that met in the next town, Dunstable, and we decided we could certainly do with help and advice from other parents. The group was small and friendly, and surprisingly I met up with a friend I had known from years ago in AFASIC. The group was run by a social worker, and chatting to him was the start of our education. He arranged for us to have a place on a course called 'Moving Forward', which was run to help people just like us. Social Services are faced with so many emergency situations when parents, not knowing what to do, or how to go about anything, just die, and leave an adult with special needs. This is very traumatic all round, and leads to a situation where Social Services spend most of their time, and money, dealing with emergencies. The 'Moving Forward' course is to help parents, and teach them what is available in the way of independent supported living. It was very informative, and we left feeling motivated. It wasn't all in a positive way in our case, as Freddie, being in full-time employment, didn't seem to be eligible for much help at all, but we knew we were the ones who had to do something.

Dad's message kept running through our heads, and we talked to Freddie as Dad had suggested. We explained the situation to him, and talked about finding him some accommodation of his own; possibly, if we could find someone to share, to get a small place for two. We were honest with him and told him how awful it would be if we both died, and left him stranded. It was such an awful thought, we told him we couldn't possibly let it happen. We would give him lots of help, and teach him slowly what he needed to know. We assured him we would be around for him, and it was better we did it now, before we became so old and silly that he was looking after us.

I had been going through a bad patch with the ME, it was winter, and it was all par for the course with my health. I had given up the line dancing as my joints couldn't take any more.

I had pushed the boundaries and found them, and although I was very disappointed about the dancing, I said how lucky I was to have had 18 months of dancing whilst having ME. It was a bright sunny afternoon, and we hadn't seen the sun for weeks, so I decided to put on my thickest clothes and go for a walk. I was heading for the Riverside Walk, the scene of so much scooter action in the past, but for no good reason I went a different way. As I walked, I saw a small terraced house that was vacant. The thought just crossed my mind that it wasn't far from home, and it was also accessible for the supermarket. It wasn't one of those sudden flashes of inspiration, it was just something in the back of my mind.

A few days later I mentioned it to John, who said, 'Well, let's go and have a look.' We both agreed it was a dear little house, in an ideal location, but how were we going to find a person to share with Freddie? Again we talked to Freddie, as Dad had advised, and Freddie said he would like to see the house. When we took him along the following Saturday he seemed very keen, and much to our surprise, said, 'Well I could move in on my own to start.' I immediately said I was willing to stay for the first couple of nights, to see how everything worked. It all seemed too good an opportunity to miss. We felt Dad's hand was at the helm, and it wasn't long before Freddie moved out from the family home.

Meanwhile Sue had taken herself to a Spiritualist meeting in Bournemouth. She was told by the medium, 'I have an elderly gentleman here who is walking with two sticks, very bent over, and shuffling along. The man then waved his false teeth in the air saying "These never fitted properly, but I don't have to wear them now." He is absolutely fine and enjoying himself, and there is music all around, playing very loudly.'

When Sue told me, we both laughed. Dad had been a terror

with his false teeth. When he lived with us I would put the fixative on them every morning, and every day he would wipe it off. They slipped down, and fell out on occasions. Every time the dentist sorted them out, Dad would customise them with a file! He loved his Salvation Army brass band music. It reminded him of his days as a band master in Battersea. He always had it turned up at full volume, so there was no change there.

15

Janice

At Easter our friends Janice and Bryan came to stay. They were always very supportive of Freddie, and wanted to see his house. Janice's cancer had returned. It had started originally as breast cancer, and she bravely agreed to very invasive surgery. She came through that, and taking medication, she had 12 years of living life to the full. Just before Christmas three years previously she had phoned to tell me the news she had never wanted to give me. Her cancer was back, and this time it was in her bones. She had 'hot spots' of it all round her body. We were terribly upset, but again Janice was determined to put up a good fight. She went through some very gruelling treatments, and surgery. She had several courses of chemotherapy, and for over three years she was unbelievably strong. Bryan and her family were very supportive, and through it all she continued to work part-time, not retiring until she had clocked up 25 years of service.

That Easter Janice was disappointed that she had to take extra rest after breakfast each day, but she looked her usual immaculate self, and her keen sense of humour was still with her. Freddie was delighted to show off his house to his Auntie Janice and Uncle Bryan. They had always been a large part of Freddie's life, as Janice and I had been friends since childhood.

Janice had brought the remains of her retirement cake, left over from her party a few days before. We all sat by the canal watching the narrow boats, drinking hot tea, and polishing off Janice's cake.

In June we were spending a week of Freddie's holiday in our favourite destination, the Isle of Wight. Janice and Bryan came across from Lymington on the ferry for the day. The weather wasn't great, but we spent a happy day together. It was the company, not the weather, that mattered. When it was time for them to go, we waved them off on the ferry. Janice stood by the big window in the lounge of the ferry and waved, and as the ferry slipped slowly out to sea we continued to wave until they were out of sight.

I never saw Janice again. In August we received a call from Bryan saying Janice was in the hospice, and it was looking likely that she only had hours to live. It was all very sudden. The next day her son phoned to say she had gone. I was devastated. I had spoken to her on the phone about a week before, and that call is now one of my treasured memories.

To say the autumn was wet was an understatement. There were floods in all parts of the country, and it felt as if it had rained every day for months. My viruses came to the fore again, and I struggled with the Christmas preparations. According to my notebook it was 6th January 2013 when I made one of my visits to the Spiritualist meeting in Leighton Buzzard. The medium was a charming young lady who came to me with the following message.

'I have a lovely lady here who passed suddenly in the end, and it was something to do with her brain. This lady took a pride in her appearance, liked nice clothes, and wore makeup.' The medium described the lady's hair. 'I feel you were almost as close as sisters. You had spent many holidays together, and over the years you had lots of laughs together. You have been missing her dreadfully, but you must understand she is in a position where she can do much more to help us. From the Spirit World she can help a lot more than on Earth. She wants you to write a book because you could help so many people. It is only lack of confidence on your part that stops you. You have the ability. You have trouble with your hands writing, but they will give you healing for that. This lady wants you to know she is often around you. You have other people around you from the Spirit World, so she wants you to know her call sign will be to touch the fringe of your hair.'

I knew this was Janice, and words can't describe how excited I was to hear from her. I couldn't wait to pick up the phone and tell Bryan. He confirmed to me that the cancer had reached her brain. I knew she had received radiotherapy to her head, but I didn't know it was her brain that had caused her death. I was shocked at the suggestion that I should write a book. Me? Write a book? Whatever was I supposed to write about?

In this book I have attempted to show how much help I have had in my life, and how the knowledge that we don't die has changed my life. I have tried to show how I have coped with the challenges I have faced. I have written about my dear dad's struggle in later life with dementia and Alzheimer's. I don't want anyone to think by portraying the funnier side of day-to-day life looking after Dad, I have been poking fun. That has not been my intention. I have had discussions with Sue as to whether to include some of the stories, or not. We are both firmly of the belief that Dad has a wonderful sense of humour, and will now be able to see the funny side of all that happened. We both have the utmost respect for Dad, and love him to pieces.

I am not a medium, and there are lots of people with far more spiritual knowledge than me. I have just wanted to write my opinions formed from my experiences. We were visiting some friends recently, people we hadn't seen for many years. The conversation was getting quite deep, and one of the friends turned to me and said, 'Where do you stand on the Bible?'

Once I had dismissed the silly image of myself standing in my bedroom, on a huge Bible, dusting the top of the wardrobe, I replied, 'I think its main message is that we don't die. There is life after death. I also think you have to bear in mind a lot of it was written after a time delay of many years, and it has been translated over and over again. A lot of it was also written to suit the politics of the time, to scare the people, and stop trouble. That doesn't mean to say you should forget the main message.'

Personally, I don't like labels. I hate the way we divide ourselves up by saying, 'You are a Baptist, you are a Catholic, you are a Muslim', and so on. I think we should all be kind to one another, look after one another as human beings, and care for the animal kingdom, and our planet. I can't understand why we divide ourselves. For me we are all human beings. My Uncle Harry was a wonderful character, full of fun and laughter, and would help anyone. He had a hard upbringing in a children's home, and he didn't have any time for any religious talk. Uncle Harry died when I was a child, and my mother asked her father, who was a Major in the Salvation Army, where he thought Uncle Harry would go. My grandfather said to my mother, 'By their fruits you shall know them.' In other words, what you do on Earth to help others denotes whether you are a good person. He was sure Uncle Harry was happily living in heaven, or as I would say, the Spirit World.

The way I make sense of it all is by believing we live many lives, and we are all given free will. By that I mean we make our own decisions. I think we make a very careful plan, or chart, for our life before we incarnate. We set out a series of challenges for ourselves, and things we need to experience to help us make good spiritual development. I believe we come to Earth in groups, and we plan very carefully who we will have around us to support us with our challenges. Most of those close to us have been with us in other lives. Your husband in this life may have been your brother, or uncle, or dare I say it, your sister, in earlier lives. I think we are helped to make our life charts, and a lot of planning goes into them.

People often ask me what I think happens when a lady dies, and she has had four husbands, who have all died before her. Will her passing into the Spirit World cause a massive punch-up between the husbands? My answer to that is, when you die your memory of past lives is restored,you know who they have been in previous lives. The lady could have been a mother, a sister, an auntie, or just a friend to them, so it is unlikely there would be any fighting! Another favourite question I am asked is about suicide. I believe we all have to review our lives, and see how well we have done, when we first pass into the Spirit World. We judge ourselves. If we feel we have failed in certain ways, we probably choose to repeat those tasks when we come again. We give ourselves a sort of 'must try harder next time' remark on our report. I do not subscribe to hellfire. I think hell is what you put yourself through if you feel you have failed. I also believe that if you have been a really wicked person, and you show no remorse, you choose to hang out with similar people in a horrible place, that I term 'Winterland'. You are always approached and given the opportunity to show remorse, but while you resist you don't make any progress.

I find it very interesting that so many 'near-death experiences' that people report, all seem to be very similar. They talk about leaving their Earthly body, and a feeling of weightlessness, and great joy as they pass through a tunnel of light. At the end of the tunnel they are told to return to Earth if it is a near-death experience. If it is your time to go home, then at the end of the tunnel a loved one extends a hand, and you are taken into a most beautiful meadow full of wild flowers, in vibrant colours. There you have a glorious reunion with your loved ones in the Spirit World, including all your pets jostling to get to you. You proceed from there to the Hall of Records, which is a beautiful marble building, where you review your life.

As I have said before, I have a burning question, 'What do they do in heaven (the Spirit World) all day?' From what I have been able to piece together from messages via mediums, I think that we can take holidays, play music, dance, join in activities with other groups of people, whatever we like. Travel is by thought, we can think ourselves where we want to be, but we also have a desire to work, to help those on Earth. We also prepare for our next incarnation. I think we can send healing. I have heard mediums saying if we want healing we must *ask* the Spirit World. In one message from my mum she talked about having a job, meeting and greeting people when they passed into the Spirit World, but these people were having trouble accepting the fact they lived on. It was her task to reassure them, and explain to them what had happened. They were usually people who had been adamant that when you were dead, you were dead. She said the things they said were quite often very funny. Judging by the number of times I have heard a medium say to me that they can hear loud Salvation Army brass band music, I think Dad is making up for his years of deafness!